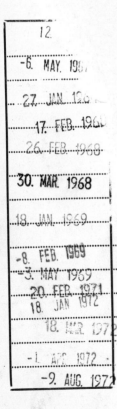

SCOTTISH COSTUME
1550–1850

PLATE I

HIGHLAND CHIEFTAIN C.1660

SCOTTISH COSTUME
1550–1850

BY

STUART MAXWELL

AND

ROBIN HUTCHISON

WITH FOUR COLOUR PLATES
AND 24 DRAWINGS BY
KATHLEEN MANN

LONDON
ADAM & CHARLES BLACK

© A. AND C. BLACK LTD 1958
4, 5 AND 6 SOHO SQUARE LONDON W.I

MADE IN GREAT BRITAIN
PRINTED BY MORRISON AND GIBB LTD.
LONDON AND EDINBURGH

CONTENTS

ILLUSTRATIONS

COLOUR PLATES

DRAWINGS

ACKNOWLEDGEMENTS

We gratefully acknowledge permission to adapt illustrations from portraits in the possession of the following :

MRS G. PURVIS-RUSSELL-MONTGOMERY
THE RT. HON. THE EARL OF ELGIN
THE ROYAL COMPANY OF ARCHERS
HIS GRACE THE DUKE OF BUCCLEUCH
LADY BIDDULPH
THE RIGHT HON. THE EARL OF MORAY
SIR JAMES HUNTER BLAIR, BT.
THE CHURCH OF SCOTLAND
MRS DALYELL OF THE BINNS
C. P. KERR, ESQ.
THE SCOTTISH NATIONAL PORTRAIT GALLERY

We are also grateful to Mrs Siddons Budgen, Mrs P. C. Smythe, The National Museum of Antiquities of Scotland and to many others for help in different ways.

FOREWORD

WE were asked to write a " non-academic " book on costume. While that does not excuse factual errors, it is our excuse for not burdening the text with footnotes giving references. The bibliography lists the principal sources ; both individual works and club series containing relevant volumes will be found there, but it is by no means a comprehensive list. Nor have we listed the manuscript sources, often giving valuable material, which we have encountered in our daily work. One result of the research for this book is the compilation of a source book of Scottish costume (in manuscript), which has been deposited in the National Museum of Antiquities and will be available for reference there. The making of it has not stopped with the publication of the book, and additions and information about sources will be welcomed.

You will not find here a complete guide enabling you to dress a play taking place in a particular year. For one thing that would need more space than we have ; for another it would need a great deal more research. We hope this book will provide a survey which will stimulate the specialist studies of particular aspects of Scottish costume through the ages which are necessary before the definitive work can be written.

Finally, there is the question of the costumes themselves.

The study of authentic Scottish costumes in museums and private collections has not yet begun. Scotland does not have a costume museum ; nor do we know of a Dr. Cunnington whose collection would start one, supposing a municipality as enlightened as Manchester could be found to house and staff it. What many readers can do is to ensure that collections and individual items of dress known to them find their way to museums and private collections where they will be preserved.

1550–1603 : INTRODUCTION

IN 1550 Scotland was in the midst of the wars and internal strife resulting from the Reformation. James V had been dead for eight years, the English army had only just been driven out with the help of French arms, and the Queen, Mary, a child, was being educated in France. The country was divided into two main factions, Roman Catholic and Protestant, the former in favour of a French, and the latter in favour of an English, alliance. Until the flight of Mary to England in 1568 and the capture of Edinburgh Castle by the Protestant Regent Morton in 1573, the civil war caused great misery in the country. From that date the country was largely at peace, though the seeds of further civil war were sown by James VI, when he followed a policy in favour of episcopacy.

Despite the civil war the country was growing in prosperity, and trade increased, until at the end of the century, Scotland was more prosperous than it had been for a very long period. The increase of wealth from trade affected the merchants and burghs, and the wealthy middle class increased. We find a complaint by Sir Richard Maitland of Lethington that " wyfes of the burroustoun " (burgh town) were dressing in the fashions of their superiors, the nobility. The increase of wealth did not, perhaps, affect the already luxurious costume of the fashionable, but it increased the number of persons who were able to afford fashionable clothes.

This was the last period in which the court, the centre of fashion, was resident in Scotland, and thus the last period in which fashionable dress was "Scottish." After the accession of James VI to the English throne, the centre of fashion moved south, and the influence was ever increasingly English.

1550–1603 : WOMEN

THE evidence available does not give a complete picture of the female styles and fashions in vogue in Scotland during this period. Though there is a great deal of information to be gathered from documents, most of it is in the form of domestic accounts and there is little descriptive matter. Portrait and other pictorial evidence is extremely meagre, and that which does exist is mainly concerned with men's costume, and with the last quarter of the century.

Two poems of the mid-sixteenth century describe the costume of ladies in Scotland, though they do not give the general shapes of the costume. Both are complaints against what the writers considered to be abuses, and thus probably describe the exaggerations rather than the " mean " of the fashion. Sir David Lyndsay (or Lindsay) of the Mount, Lord Lyon King of Arms and poet, writing before 1542, complains about the long trailing gowns worn by women, the trains of which throw up dust and become caked with dirt. This long train, " syde tailles " (side tails), Lindsay calls them, was in imitation of the court robes of the queen, and was worn by all classes, much to the poet's disgust, even by the serving women, " Quhilk has skant twa markis for thair feis " (who have scarcely two marks for their wages), and whose clothes were made of undyed wool.

> " I think it is ane verray scorne,
>   That every lady of the land
>   Suld have hir taill so syde trailland (trailing so long behind them) ;
>   Howbeit thay bene of hie estait
>   The Quene thay suld nocht counterfait ;
>   Quhare ever thay go, it may be sene,
>   How kirk, and calsay (street) thay soup (sweep) clene . . ."

He remarks how they had to carry their trains to keep them from the mud, and adds a dig at the Church :

> " Bot, I lauch (like) best to se ane Nwn (nun),
>   Gar beir hir taill abone hir bun (have to carry her
>   tail above her bum)
>   For no' thing ellis, as I suppois,
>   Bot for to schaw hir lillie quhyte hois (white hose)."

Sir Richard Maitland of Lethington, writing a little later, probably about 1550, also complains about women spending money in their desire to keep up with the new fashions, the constant complaint of men commenting on the fashions of their womenfolk. Maitland does not confine himself to one aspect of female dress, but describes and blasts all the female fashions. He complains with Lindsay about the long trains, and also mentions that long hanging sleeves " lyk geill poikkes " (jelly bags) were also worn. The gowns were trimmed with velvet at the sleeve, neck and train. Their outer skirts and cloaks were of silk, the latter adorned with fur. Their petticoats were embroidered with rich braid, and decorated with ribbon. Again appears the complaint that the women lifted their gowns when walking

" to schaw thair wylicot (petticoat) hingand doun," or like Lindsay's nun " sumtyme bayth thay will upbeir to schaw thair hoiss (hose) of blak or broun," the hose being of silk. Here also appears the complaint that the search for fashion led the women to dress " above their station " :

> " I mein of thame thair honour dreidis,
>   Quhy (why) sould thay not have honeist weidis (clothes)
> To thair estait doand effeir (suited to their estate) ?
> I mein of thame thair stait exceidis
> And all for newfangilnes of geir."

The general shape of the gown was a long tight bodice, a tight sleeve with a long trailing edge, and a full skirt which was elongated to a train, but not hooped. The neckline was probably square in most cases. The sleeves may have been separate, as they were in England at this period ; references to them as separate articles appear in accounts.

The hats, according to Maitland, were of velvet, worn high on the head and decorated with gold thread. His reference does not make their form clear, but two types appear in illustrative material of a later date, either a high crowned felt hat with a narrow brim, or a flat round cap with a tiny brim, similar to the man's head-dress in Fig. 1, but slightly higher in the crown. The wearing of a hat seems to have been the only differentiation between the middle class and the nobility who affected a velvet hood :

> " Between thame, and nobillis of blude,
>   Na difference bot ane velwet huid."

The Lord High Treasurer's Accounts give the cost and details of preparing garments for a lady of the court. In 1551, an outfit was made for Lord Governor Arran's daughter, when she was presented to Mary of Lorraine :

" deliverit to the quenis tailyeour to be ane goune to My Lord Governouris doichter :—

5 elnis gray welwett (velvet)	£17 10s.
2 elne gray taffiteis (taffeta) to lyne the samyn (same)	£1 12s.
2 elnis gray to lyne this goune and ane gowne of figurate welwett gottin furtht (taken from) my Lord Governouris gardrope (wardrobe)	10s.
2 elnis of bukcrame to bouster (pad or stiffen) thir gounes with	6s.
3 quarteris (of an ell) small canves to lyne the bodeis of the samyn	2s. 6d.
2 elnis blak taffite of foure threddis to lyne the goune of fygurett welwett witht .	£1 12s."

The " small " (fine) canvas was used to stiffen the bodice of the gown, perhaps in lieu of any sort of foundation garment, mention of which does not appear as early as this. The Account goes on to describe the accessories to go with the gowns :

" deliverit to the said tailyeour :—

4 elnis satin to be hir 4 hudis (hoods) & 4 pair of slevis (sleeves) viz. ane elne crammesy satin	£3 10s.
2 elnis bukrame to lyne thir hudis	8s.
2 elnis taffiteis of 4 threddis to lyne the saidis hudis and sleves	£1 12s.
for wyre to thir hudis	6d.
3 elnis ribben silk to cover the wyre of the hudis	3s. 6d.
Ane elne and ane quarter bred reid (bright red ?) to be to hir ane vylecoit (petticoat)	£1 15s."

Details of other gowns follow, and the purchase of more

" braid reid " to make hose, and of silk to be " ane tippett " (shawl), bartane cloth for sarkis (shirts) and fine linen for collars.

Fur was used both for warmth and decoration. Arran gave Lady Gordon, who was convalescing at Linlithgow, a wyliecoat trimmed with fur, " quhite lamb skynnis."

One of the earliest portraits (1561) of a Scottish lady of noble blood, is the Hans Eworth of Agnes, wife of the Earl of Moray, Mary Queen of Scots' half-brother. Though presumably painted outside Scotland, the costume shown is probably that worn in the north. The gown is black, with the appearance of silk, banded vertically with velvet braid. The bodice, which is very close fitting, has a high neckline, and a high standing collar, edged with fur. The sleeves, which are puffed out at the shoulder and fit closely to the arm, reach to just above the elbow and terminate in narrow fur cuffs. The waist is low, and though the portrait is only half-length, enough of the skirt shows to make it obvious that while it is full it is not hooped. Under the gown Lady Moray wears a white garment, the " sark " mentioned in the Treasurer's Accounts, probably made of fine linen. This has a high collar, open at the front, with a ruff edge which encircles the neck, just below the ears, and frames the lower half of the face. The cuffs have broad stiff frills at the wrist. Both ruff and cuffs are decorated with broderie anglaise. Between the wrist and the cuff of the gown, the sark is covered with an over-sleeve of open black net, which shows the white beneath it.

On her head she wears a tight-fitting cap, which covers the back of the head, reaching the ears at the sides and coming to a slight peak high on the forehead (the Mary, Queen of Scots, cap). This is decorated with a line of jewels, which runs from ear to ear. A heavy jewel is worn at the throat, and a double gold cord is wound twice round the neck, and loosely knotted. Except for the jewellery, the scheme is one of black relieved by the white of the sark.

Between 1560 and 1580 or –90, dark colours, particularly black, were worn by both men and women, and it may have been that this was the result of the influence of the Reformed Church, whose power was at its highest during the minority of James VI. An inventory of the goods and gear belonging to the " Umquhile Dame Elizabeth Ross, Lady Fleming," includes a number of articles of clothing, the majority of which are black or dark in colour. A few items are more elaborate, and must have been rich in appearance : " Ane goun of cramasie welnot (velvet) wit ane bodie (bodice) but (without) slaves (sleeves) pasmentit (decorated) with gold and silver " and " ane goun of quhit (white) satein wit ane bodie but slaves pasmentit wt clayt (cloth) of gold."

Towards the end of the period, the gown lost its relatively simple style, and became more exaggerated and elaborate. The bodice elongated, and lost its relation to the body inside it. It became long and thin, with a low waistline dipping to a point at the level of the loins. This bodice was heavily stiffened, and at the end of the period resembled an inverted cone. The skirts became fuller and fuller, till they had to be supported by the farthingale (hooped petticoat). The sleeves altered and became long and full, padded out in an exaggerated form (Fig. 1).

The hair style also changed at the end of the century ; until this time the hair had been drawn back from the forehead and was covered by a hat or cap, but in the 1590s, the hair began to appear as a decorative feature in itself, either showing below the cap or entirely uncovered, waved

and piled on the head. This change may have had two
origins, either the influence of Anne of Denmark, whose hair
is shown uncovered in most portraits, or the influence of the
English court.

The costume so far described was that which was
" fashionable," but it is likely, as in later periods, that even
the most noble of ladies used homespuns and home produced
linen for everyday or domestic wear, and the lower middle
class and working classes had to rely on the coarsest of
materials for their wants.

The wages of the period were so low that the average
servant must have been hard put to it even to make her own
clothes. A maid in Elgin was paid 8s. in money for about
six months' wages in 1572, and in the same year and in the
same town a yard and a quarter of coarse material cost
7s. 6d., and two years later a shirt " lost in the wash " was
valued at 6s. The servant relied on cast-off clothing belonging
to her employers, and indeed they were part of the regular
wage. The entry referred to in the Burgh Court records of
Elgin, gives the details of a servant's contract, " Mage
Pakman, spous to Henre Froster, was decernit (ordered) to
pay to " Issabell Kemp, servand, aucht s. (8s.) monie
thre quarteris [of an ell] harn cleith and ane half eln lynning
cleith, ane pair mendit (mended) schone and oldren (old)
sark for his fie and buntays (bounties) in service making to
saidis Henre and Mage betwix the feistis of Vitsonday and
Martimes (Martinmas) last bypast."

Shoes were perhaps the cheapest article, one of Scotland's
main items of production being leather. The price of shoes
was controlled by the Burgh in Elgin until the early
eighteenth century. In 1571 " menis shone [to be sold]
for thre shillings, and the wemen['s] schone for tua shillings

of the best thai (they) haif and the secunder of minor price." In 1578 the prices were the same, and the prices of children's shoes are listed, " bairnis [shoes to cost] 1s. 6d. thay being of saxtein zeir (years) auld, and gif thai be of les age nor tuelf zeiris auld the schone for sic (such) bairnis to be sauld for 1s."

The leather shoes were worn by all classes, varying only in quality. The fashionable would also wear velvet shoes with their rich gowns. The actual form is difficult to establish, but most shoes appear to have been " slipper " in style, and perhaps decorated with a knot of ribbons. No mention is made of lacing shoes for women.

For outdoor wear the lady of fashion wore what was called a cloak, but it would be more accurate to describe it as a coat, for, at any rate at the beginning of the period, it had the same long hanging sleeves as the gown, and in the inventory of Lady Fleming mentioned above such a garment is described as a " coat." To judge from the same inventory the outer garment could be intended for decoration as well as cover : " ane coit of purpour welvat (purple velvet) pasmentit with gold and silver." These garments were made with or without a hood attached. The hoods mentioned above in the Lord High Treasurer's Accounts were probably the court headgear as described in the portrait of the Countess of Moray. The hood worn in conjunction with the outdoor garment was larger and enveloped the whole head (Fig. 1).

Lindsay mentions (with adverse comment) the custom of women using a kerchief to veil their faces when in the streets and even in kirk. From his description this was worn over the face leaving only the eyes visible in the same manner as Muslim women are veiled. This practice seems to have been dying out in the last half of the century, for few mentions

I. GENTLEMAN IN COURT DRESS, 1558   LADY, 1593

are made of it.   This veil may have been the forerunner of
the pinner which was the almost universal form of everyday
wear in the following century, and indeed the kerchief was
probably worn over the head and the loose end drawn across
the face.

Neither the cloak nor coat with a hood affected the use
of the plaid, which appears regularly in the accounts
available.   There is no evidence to suppose that its distribu-
tion or method of arrangement was any different from
later centuries, and it is certain that it was worn by all
classes, except when the most fashionable garments were
being worn.   Little indication is given of the materials used
for making women's plaids, but most were of wool differing
only in quality, colour and design.   The mention of tartan
in accounts is not so frequent as in the later centuries.

1550–1603 : MEN

THOUGH accounts, both domestic and official (those of the
Lord High Treasurer), dealing with the purchase of male
clothing are more extensive than those dealing with that of
women, descriptive material is almost non-existent, and no
poet thought fit to satirize the male, as Lindsay and Maitland
did the female.   On the other hand there is more pictorial
evidence available of male costume, though again this is
very slight compared with the mass of portraits available
for later periods.   It is obvious from the accounts of purchases,
however, that the male noble purchased a far greater
proportion of his wardrobe made-up than his wife.   For

while the wife purchased materials and a few rich gowns complete, the husband bought many everyday garments as well as those of a more luxurious nature.

It is difficult to draw an accurate picture of the male costume at the beginning of the period, but it consisted of doublet and breeches reaching to just below the knees. It is necessary to point out to those studying this period, that that garment described as hose in the sixteenth century is the same as the " breeks " or breeches of the seventeenth century. The stockings, called hose in the seventeenth and subsequent centuries, are generally described as " shanks " in the sixteenth century. The word " shanks " survived for a long time but gradually gave way to the anglicized " hose."

Throughout this period the doublet changed little except in detail. It was a close fitting garment which buttoned up to the neck and followed the lines of the body. The sleeves were of the same nature, fitting to the arm down its whole length. The main variations were in the collar, the shoulders and the waist.

The collar was largely conditioned by the fashion of the shirt and its neck decoration. Early in the period the shirt ended in a plain band, and the doublet had a very small stand-up collar and in some pictorial representations, no collar at all. By the 1560s, the shirt developed a decorated collar, and the doublet a tall, stiff, stand-up collar, which reached to the ears, dipping slightly below the chin, where it was left open down to the top button of the doublet itself. This fashion prevailed for some time, but as the collar of the shirt developed into a ruff, so the collar of the jacket closed in front and became lower to accommodate the ruff. As the ruff became larger and more horizontal, so the collar

of the doublet became less and less obtrusive, until at the
end of this period it had almost disappeared.

The waistline of the doublet started low, at the beginning
of the period, just above the hips and dipping slightly at
the front. This dip varied a great deal, being more pronounced in more fashionable garments, and almost non-
existent in everyday wear. As the period progressed,
the dip became more and more pronounced, until it reached
almost to the groin, and, together with the padding of the
doublet, it produced a Punch-like shape to the figure.

The shoulder line also changed slightly during the
fifty years under discussion. In the 1550s the natural line
of the shoulder was in no way changed. The doublet,
though in most cases padded, followed the natural line
from the base of the neck to the point of the shoulder, but
by the end of the century the join between sleeve and body
was often decorated by an epaulette, varying in form but
often consisting of a series of small overlapping flaps. This
decoration altered the natural shape of the shoulders,
giving it a square outline. This fashion, though it lasted
well into the next century, was in no way universal. It is
interesting to note that this " squaring " of the shoulder,
now so much part of the tailor's art, disappears almost
entirely in the mid-seventeenth century, reappearing only
in comparatively modern times. Throughout the late
seventeenth and eighteenth centuries, no attempt was made
to give the male " powerful " shoulders.

During the whole period the doublet was worn very
short, only just covering the top of the breeches, a matter
of a few inches. The skirt of the doublet below the waistline
was very narrow, sometimes plain, but often made of overlapping flaps.

The breeches show perhaps the greatest change of all, for though the actual form, a full garment, with the legs tapering to below the knee, remained constant, their proportions varied greatly, thus changing the whole balance and appearance of the figure. In the 1550s the breeches were full, lined but apparently not padded, but by the end of the century the garment had become enormous, stuffed with hair or wool, so that the hips were often one and a half times as wide as the shoulders.

There was, in England, a variation of the breeches described above. These also were stuffed to absurd widths, but reached to only half-way down the thigh. They do appear in at least one " court " portrait of a Scottish sitter of the late 1550s, but were probably not universal. The portrait is of the fifth Lord Seton (Fig. 1), in the dress of the Master of the Queen's Household, but this portrait was almost certainly painted in France, and probably represents a French rather than a Scottish fashion. The other well-known " Scottish " example of this fashion is the double portrait of Lord Darnley and his brother in Holyroodhouse, but again this portrait was painted in the south before Darnley came to Scotland. Both these portraits show the short form of breeches, only varying in material and minor design : in both the breeches are gathered to the leg well above the knee. The portrait of Lord Seton which can be dated as having been painted in the late 1550s, shows that the breeches incorporate a codpiece, a variation which appears in no other Scottish portrait we have seen.

For court dress, an additional garment was worn over the doublet. This was a short cloak or cape which reached to the hips, with or without a collar. This cape was probably tailored to fit on the shoulders and is normally shown open in front, to reveal the doublet. It was part of the " suit " rather than an additional garment for outdoor wear, for which purpose a heavier and longer garment was worn.

One of the earliest pictorial representations of male dress of this period is the memorial relief to Edward Maxwell, dated 1568, which is reproduced in the Royal Commission on Ancient Monuments Inventory of Kirkcudbright. It is of particular interest, as it shows the costume of a country laird rather than noble or a member of the court. The carving is very simple and, unfortunately, little detail can be seen, but the general cut of the garments is clear. The doublet is cut to fit the body with no paddings or exaggerations, and even the waistline lacks the fashionable dip in the front and runs horizontally very low round the body. The skirt of the doublet is very short, and is slightly peaked at the front, which achieves, in a simpler way, the dipping waist of the more fashionable garments, and it has a rudimentary collar, little more than an edging, round the hole for the neck. The breeches are full but do not appear to be " stuffed," and reach to below the knee. Below these, Maxwell wears stockings (shanks) and shoes. Unfortunately the modelling of this piece of sculpture is so simplified that mechanics of the shoes cannot be discovered, and though no lacing or buckling is shown the shape of the shoes suggests that something of this sort was necessary. The shoes reach well up the ankle, both front and back, and are in the nature of half-boots, fitting closely to foot and ankle, which makes it appear that they could not be removed without being undone in some way.

In contrast, the portrait of Lord Seton mentioned above (Fig. 1) shows court dress of the most extravagant sort.

This, as has been pointed out, owed much to foreign influences, but as it depicts the sitter as Master of the Queen's Household *c.* 1558, it must have been worn in this country.

The doublet differs from the general design in that it is secured only for the top few inches at the neck and falls away to the waist. The edges of the doublet curve back to the line of the waist and the skirt is cut away on each side. This doublet is worn over another garment, which shows between the front edges. The collar is a vertical one ; the top few inches are allowed to bend over, and are topped by the white collar of the shirt. The breeches are very wide, reaching to above the knee, and are constructed of panels tapering to the waist, with, as has been mentioned, the unusual addition of a codpiece. Lord Seton wears an elaborate cloak over the doublet with a high stand-up collar. The material is of the richest, and the applied decoration indicates the position the sitter holds as Master of the Queen's Household. The whole suit is embroidered with the Scots thistle, and his staff has Mary, Queen of Scots' initial surmounted by the crown.

Another portrait of about the same date is that of the Regent Moray by Hans Eworth, dated 1561, and companion to the one described in the women's section of this period. This portrait shows an interesting contrast to Lord Seton's : though the materials are rich, the colour is sombre, and it is possible that this indicates that those nobles who supported the reformers wore clothes of a more sombre hue than the supporters of the Royal party. The doublet is much the same in cut as the one depicted in Edward Maxwell's effigy : it is buttoned from the neck to the waist, which dips at the front. The collar is high, and stands up vertically, rising higher at the back of the head to the level of the centre of the ears, and dipping to just below the chin at the front. This collar is sufficiently wide to allow it to be lined with the ruffled edge of the shirt collar, which frames the lower half of the face. The suit, which is black, with the appearance of silk, is decorated with vertical stripes of another black material, probably velvet, which converge slightly at the waist. A short row of buttons, spherical in shape, close the neck, and the whole front of the doublet is decorated with pairs of the same buttons. The portrait is half length, which does not allow the bottom of the doublet to be seen, but sufficient does show to indicate that the waistline dips to a peak at the front. A short cloak, also black and striped in the same manner as the doublet, is hung over the shoulder, but — unlike the Seton portrait—has no collar and is much more meagre in cut, giving the impression that it would not meet acrosss the front of the body. It is secured by two lengths of gold chain, with circular links, fastened just below the collar.

It is in portraits of the late 1560s and early 1570s that the change in the proportions of the breeches begins to show, and two portraits in the Scottish National Portrait Gallery show the beginnings of the development. These portraits are of James VI as a boy and of the Earl of Morton, both painted in the early 1570s, and both by the same artist, probably a Fleming working in Scotland. The breeches shown in both portraits are heavily padded, so that the hip and thigh of the wearer are greatly exaggerated, the outside edge coming out from the waist almost horizontally. The leg then tapers down to below the knee, where it is gathered in the normal way. The accounts of the period do not indicate

how these garments were padded, but in England horse or
other animal hair was used. A satirical poem of the end of
the century is entitled, " A Lamentable Complaint of the
pore countryman against great Hose for the losse of their
cattelles Tails." The poor man who narrates the poem
complains that the rich

> " . . . to furnyshe forthe theare pryde [stuff their breeches]
>   With woole, with flax, with hare also
>   to make thear bryches wide . . ."

Some historians relate that this fashion was originated
by James VI, who feared assassination by stabbing. This
is obviously false, as the fashion was well established when
James was a boy.

At the same time as this·change appears in the breeches,
so the doublet changes, from a garment with applied
decoration to a quilted one.

The portrait of the Earl of Morton shows this type of
costume in some detail. The doublet, although padded,
still follows the line of the body as in the early portraits
described, though a line of piping round the join of the
sleeve shows the beginnings of the epaulette. The doublet
buttons up to the neck, with a short collar rather higher at
the back than at the front, so that the circular ruff rises to
the level of the ears at the back and frames the face. The
waist dips at the front, and there is no skirt to the doublet
visible. The quilting is made up of horizontal bands,
divided by double lines of stitching, each decorated with
diagonal slashes, running in opposite directions in each
adjoining segment. The quilting on the sleeves is similarly
decorated and also horizontal.

The breeches are immense, spreading to about one and a

quarter times the breadth of the shoulder at their widest point. No decoration or slashing is visible and the material, though black like the doublet, is probably plain.

The general effect is even more sombre than the portrait of the Earl of Moray. The whole costume is black ; even the row of spherical buttons closing the doublet are covered in black material, the only relief the white of the linen shirt at neck and cuffs and the belt, which is lightly decorated with gold or silver.

The portrait of James VI as a child is almost exactly similar in design, except that the breeches are not quite so exaggerated, and the quilting of the body is in vertical bands, though those on the arm are horizontal. The dip of the waist is also slightly less apparent, though a narrow, gold decorated belt does show that this was an integral part of the shape of the doublet.

This costume persisted until the end of the period, indeed until well into the seventeenth century only minor changes are apparent. A portrait of Duncan Campbell of Glenorchy, dated 1601, shows very little basic difference. The high collar has disappeared and a plain white turnover collar replaces the ruff ; the quilting has disappeared, but the general cut of the doublet remains the same. The most pronounced change is in the shoulder line. The shoulder has a deep epaulette running round the joint of the sleeve and body of the doublet. The colour scheme is sombre, but slight relief is achieved by metal buttons, which decorate not only the front but also the epaulettes and the arm.

Throughout the period stockings and shoes were normal wear, though long boots were purchased for use when on horseback. The colour of both shoes and stockings would depend on the general colour scheme of the costume.

Two types of headgear were in use during the period ; the one, a form of cap (Fig. 1), was most popular in fashionable circles in the early part, while the other, a high crowned hat with a brim, became popular later in the century. However, both hats and caps were in use at the same time. In the carving of Edward Maxwell mentioned above, the figure wears a broad-rimmed hat with a conical crown, little higher than a modern bowler, while the portraits of the Earl of Moray and Lord Seton show the cap being worn. The height of the crown of the hat increased. Morton is shown wearing a hat which must have been a foot or more in height, and portraits of James VI painted in the 1590s show him wearing similar hats, very tall with conical crowns, generally decorated with an elaborate badge.

The accounts of the period give an idea of the amounts and qualities of materials used to make these garments. The most valuable group of records is the Accounts of the Lord High Treasurer which detail the costs of purchasing the materials and making the court clothes at the beginning of the period.

In 1551 purchases were made to make an outfit for the Regent, the Earl of Arran, which give a very good idea of the materials necessary for a doublet and breeches :

" Item deliverit to Archibald Dewar
    to be ane doublett to my lord
    governour, 3 elnis, quarter & half
    quarter blak satin of Wenys (40s.
    the ell)   £6 15 0
Item 3½ elnis quhite fustiane to lyne
    the samyn (6s. the ell)   £1 1s.
Item for buttonis and stenting
    (stiffening) canves to the samyn   8s.

Item 2 elnis blak welwett to be theis
    (thighs) of hois (breeches) to his
    grace (£3 10 0 the ell)   £7
Item 7 quarteris blak taffiteis to lyne
    the samyn (16s. the ell)   £1 8s.
Item 5 quarters stemmyng of Myllane
    to be schankis to the samin (40s.
    the ell)   £2 10s.
Item for cantailzeis and sewing silk
    to the theis of thir hois   £1 4s."

The reference to the thighs and " shanks " of the hose
suggests that both stockings and breeches may have been
incorporated in one garment, but the amount and type of
material, velvet lined with taffeta for the thighs alone show
that the top half of the garment was fairly bulky.

Black was not the only colour worn, because the next
entry, also in favour of the Regent Arran, is for grey velvet
to make " hois " and a little later white fustian is bought
to line a silk doublet. Details are also give of a cloak :—

" Item deliverit to Archebald Dewar
    to be ane cloik and ane coit to my
    Lord governour 5½ elnis fyne
    stemmynge of Myllane   £10 9s.
Item 2¼ elnis fyne blak satyn to
    bordour this cloik and coit   £4 10 0
Item 5 unce of Paris silk to styk the
    samyn   £2 5s.
Item 6½ elnis blak fustiane to lyne
    this coit   £2 12s
Item ane quarter of taffite of foure
    threddis to lyne the breistis of the
    samyn   4s.
Item for buttonis and buckrame to
    be peuchis (pockets) to the samyn   6s."

The above presumably refers to the making of a short
cape and a larger overgarment for outdoor wear.

An entry in the same year refers to another garment of which there is no pictorial evidence surviving : this is the nycht-goune (nightgown), not sleeping wear, but a form of housecoat worn indoors for comfort. The name and the garment survived well into the nineteenth century, and illustrations of its later form are not uncommon. Perhaps the best known is the portrait of Sir David Wilkie by Andrew Geddes, which is in the Scottish National Portrait Gallery and has often been illustrated and exhibited. The entry suggests that the earlier form differed little from those of the eighteenth and nineteenth centuries.

" Item 5 elnis lylis wirset (worsted) deliverit to the said Archebald [Dewar] to be ane nycht goune to my lord governouris sone David — £3 10s.

Item ½ ell welwett to walt the samyn — 35s.

Item buckrame to the samyn — 2s.

Item to Johnne Craig, furreour, for furring of the samyn — £2 10s.

An account rendered to the Thane of Cawdor by a tailor in 1591 gives details of more homely garments and illustrates the change of fashion in the shoulders of the doublet. The account includes " 7 quarteris of Londun claith to be your maisterchip cott———. thrie ell and ane half of fustian—ane ell of spanyeis taifty (Spanish taffeta)—half ell of stiffing gray to your M.[astership's] doublat schoulderis."

The costume of the middle and working classes can only be guessed at, little or no pictorial evidence is available, and documentary evidence is very slight. Such references as do exist make it clear that the same garments were in use, but naturally the quality of material was much poorer, coarse, homespun woollens taking the place of the silks and velvets of the richer classes. Colours were in all

probability drab, and undyed material often worn, though
an entry in the Records of Inverness Burgh Court in 1573
does refer to " ane coit " (coat) of tartan.

As in the case of women servants, so men employed in
the house, shop or on an estate were paid only a very small
part of their wages in money : the rest they received in
kind. Meal, cloth and clothing were normal items received.
The cloth would be coarse woollens or linens produced on
the estate or in the home which employed them. Clothing
might be new or especially made for a favoured servant,
but the majority received at least part of their wages in
cast-off clothing. In 1573 a dispute about wages was
settled in the Burgh Court of Elgin, and Wm Aldcorn
was ordered to pay to Thomas Air " XVIIs, IIIId monye,
twa castyng (cast-off) coittis, twa pairis castyng hois, four
castyng sarkis (shirts) and ane pair new schoin (shoes) for
the said Thomas fee and buntais (bounties) in serving the
said William ane zeir (year) bypast."

The one garment which was worn by the working and
lower middle-class men which distinguished them from their
richer fellow-countrymen was the plaid. At this period,
there is no mention that the rich wore this garment. It
normally consisted of five ells of double width woollen
material. As in later periods it was not necessarily made of
tartan, and might be of any colour or design. No evidence
exists as to the method of wear, but we think it can be
presumed that the " fashion " was no different to that of later
centuries. In wet or cold weather it was draped over head
or shoulders to cover the whole body, and when not in use
rolled and worn over one shoulder, perhaps with the ends
tied bandoleer fashion. It should be stressed that this in
no way replaced the doublet and trousers, and as far as the

C—3

lowlander was concerned was an outdoor garment in place of an " overcoat " or cloak.

The highlanders wore the same size of plaid, but in their case it did replace the breeches, and was belted at the waist. The details of this form of costume are given in the section on highland dress.

The headgear of the poorer classes was probably the bonnet, the traditional head covering of the poorer Scot. Records of its use in the seventeenth century abound, and we presume that it was worn in the late sixteenth. The bonnet has remained unchanged in essential design until modern times, though it is now most commonly called the tam-o'-shanter.

Arms of one sort or another were carried by most men of every class. This custom led to frequent affrays in the streets, and at least one Burgh, Elgin, attempted to regulate the custom. The town council records show that the following resolution was passed in 1580 : " Siclyk it is statut that nedir freman nor onfreman within this burgh in na tymes cuming sall beir or weir, jak, pleit slewes (sleeves of plate), culvering, dag, pistoll nor suord upon tham within the said burgh without speciall leceans (licence) of the provest and bailzeis and [the] maist part of the counsall."

1603   660 : INTRODUCTION

THE first thirty years after the Union of the Crowns was a period of relative peace and gradual development in Scotland. The ever-present threat of war with England, which had been the bane of Scottish life for the previous centuries, had apparently disappeared, and the internal troubles caused by the aftermath of the Reformation and the minority of the King had died down. Trade increased with the south and overseas, and though the patronage of the Court had disappeared, the majority of the nobility were still resident in Scotland. Indeed the move south of the King may have improved the trade of the merchants dealing in clothing. The centre of fashion was still the Court, though it was outside the country, and the wealthy still maintained an interest in Court fashions, going to local merchants for the materials to imitate those fashions. The new Court was infinitely richer than the old one, and finer materials were sought and imported to satisfy the demand.

From the late 'thirties until the early 1650s the whole country was racked by war. The towns suffered from occupation and, in some cases, as Dundee, from looting and destruction by opposing forces. There was a continual drain on the resources and materials to provide the armies raised by the nation, which caused definite shortages and a rise in prices. Many of the nobility and richer merchants used and lost their wealth supporting either the King or the opposition. Thus the nation, which had started the century with what seemed a promising era of peace and prosperity, was reduced by the 1650s to penury and was occupied by foreign troops. This occupation by the Commonwealth forces produced a period of peace which relieved the nation, but the damage had been great, and in 1660 the country was still recovering.

The effects of the war on fashion are difficult to determine, and the written accounts of the period are mainly factual rather than descriptive. The portraits, on the other hand, do show a change in general design from extravagance to simplicity, and though this may be the natural see-saw of fashion development, it was probably influenced by the scarcity of money to use on luxuries.

1603–1660 : WOMEN

WHEN James VI succeeded to the English throne in 1603, Scotland ceased to have a Royal Court within her own boundaries, and since that time there have been only two occasions when such a court returned for any length of time. The first was the short period of about twelve months, 1649–1650, when Charles II returned to Scotland, and the second was the Vice-regal Court of James, Duke of York, when he was Commissioner in Scotland for about two years. The move of the Court south affected the whole development of fashion in Scotland, for from this time those who wished to be in the mode turned to the south for inspiration, and letters show that an ever-increasing interest was shown

in what was " à la mode " in London. In 1614 the Countess
of Eglinton was corresponding with Jean Ruthven in Whitehall, asking for furniture and articles of clothing, and the
latter replies in one of her letters, " and as for the lace to be
a band and cuffs, and square with long peaks, pleas your
ladyship know that it is not the fashion to weare such now
and therfore I have boght such a one as all doo use at court ;
such a one directly as my mistress wears of the best Flanders
lace I could get." For a long time it was only the nobility
and those who had direct contact with the south who
followed the Court fashions, but in time the middle and
working classes imitated the nobility until by the nineteenth
century practically all the national flavour of the clothing of
the northern kingdom had been lost.

Though there are many portraits and engravings of this
period, it is difficult to be exact in describing the changes of
fashion, at any rate in female costume. Apparently many
different " fashions " were worn at the same time, and it is
possible only to indicate the general trends and major
changes in shape and style. This state of affairs existed in
both Scotland and England. The multiplicity of modes in
the south is illustrated by Wenceslas Hollar in his " Ornatus
Muliebris Anglicanus," published in 1640, where he shows
different forms of female attire. And Sir William Brereton
visiting Scotland in 1636 remarks that " Touching the fashion
of the citizens [of Edinburgh], the women here wear and
use, upon festival days, six or seven several habits and
fashions, some for distinction of widows, wives and maids,
others apparalled according to their own humour and
phantasy."

The whole seventeenth century shows a change in both
female and male costume, from elaboration to comparative

simplicity, from the highly decorated and padded garments of the early years to the simple linen and plain materials in vogue about 1700.

In 1603 the fashion in the south, and thus within a few years that of the nobility of Scotland, was a legacy from the Elizabethan Court, in which the female figure was stylized. The costume itself was a thing of beauty, but was so stuffed and boned that it had little relation to the figure within it. The upper half of the body was encased in a long, pointed stomacher very stiffly boned, which reached from a round neckline tapering down to a point at the loins. This bodice was so tight and stiff that the body had the appearance of an inverted cone. The lower half of the dress consisted of a vast array of skirt or skirts, hooped or stuffed, until in some cases it appears as an enormous drum into which the cone appears to be thrust. The sleeve was generally padded, but followed the line of the arm closely, and sometimes was decorated with a single slash, down the front, caught together at several points.

The actual dress appears to be in two parts, the bodice and a skirt, split down the front and worn over an underskirt. From the shoulders a train was worn, of the same material as the bodice, which reached almost to the ground and was in fact probably part of the dress. And worn over the dress was a sort of surcoat, often of black, but occasionally of richer fabric. This garment was sleeveless, just showing at the shoulder, and only meeting at the waist to fall away leaving the front half of the skirt exposed to view. The neck was round and low cut, but certainly in the case of older women the bust was covered with lace or gauze, part of the shift or undergarment. The evidence of portraits and family accounts of the times emphasizes the richness of the material used. A court gown would be made of a silk material in rich colours, often with added decoration of embroidery, and gold or silver lace, with elaborate buttons and bows of ribbon.

An account rendered to the Thane of Cawdor by an Edinburgh tailor in 1616, details the materials for a gown of some simplicity : " Item delyverit to James Mowat at your M[aster's] dochteris gown 13 ell of reid and blew growdgraine at 53/4 the ell ; item 9 unce fyve drop of waltingis and silk to hir gown at 40/- the unce, 9 quarteris of gray bukkasie at ane merk the ell : item twa ell of bukkram at ane merk the ell ; item 3 dusone of buttons therto 10/- ; 8 ell of balling at 3s. the ell ; item 3 quarteris of tueidill to lyne the sleives at 13/4 the ell ; item 3 quarteris and a half of yellow stennyng to be to hir twa pair of schankis (stockings) at £3 10s. the ell . . ." The buckram, and the tueidill (? tweed) was for stiffening and padding. The cost seems exhorbitant, but the prices are given in £ Scots not sterling, the rate of exchange being £12 Scots to the £1 sterling at this time. This was a fairly simple gown, for the material was presumably grogram, but other accounts of the period show more lavish materials.

All this was worn over the shift, the standard under-garment of this and later periods. It was a long-sleeved garment, decorated at neck and wrists with lace. The decoration at the wrist was a wide band of lace which turned back over the sleeve of the dress to a depth of about six inches. The material of the shift was cut away at the neck to conform with the shape of the gown, but this gap was replaced by gauze or lace, split in the middle so that the edges just touched. This was connected to a ruff, either in the shape of a wheel or a fan, the latter wired or starched to make it stand up behind the head. In the same account mentioned above, is the following item : " To hir (your M. dochter) ane fyne wyre."

The skirt was supported by the farthingale, a frame of hoops, and the upper part of the body was constricted by a bodice stiffened with whalebone. Expenses incurred by a lady of the Eglinton family in 1603 while she was at the Court in London included " ane par of quhallbon bodis, the on[e] syd with taffetie, and the oder syd with small canvos 20/-, and ane vardingell coverit with taffitie 20/-."

This very exaggerated form of costume had modified by the 1620s, and some indications of a movement towards a more natural line became apparent. The upper half of the body, though still controlled by a stiffened bodice, had lost a lot of its pointed and elongated look, and though the waistline still dipped to a point at front and back it was not so exaggerated. The skirt was still very full but fell in more gentle and natural folds, and the sleeve became rather fuller and looser, and the slash more exaggerated. (Fig. 2) shows an example of this stage of the development. The gown is made of a heavy, dark, embroidered material, possibly velvet, and the decoration in gold thread. The waist is fairly high, and the upper part of the body has some relation to a natural shape. The sleeves have a single slash and were gathered at the elbow joint and the wrist, and show underneath either a lining or the shift of white. The epaulette type of shoulder decoration, which was very prevalent, is obvious, and a cape or train, part of the dress, falls from the shoulders. By this time the Elizabethan form of the ruff had disappeared, and the broad lace collar had taken its place. The child wears a form which was most popular. The front edges of the shift, which are decorated

2. LADY AND CHILD, 1620

with lace, lie back over the neckline of the dress and a collar of lace, starched or stiffened with a wire, forms a fan behind the head. The mother's collar is fundamentally the same, except that the front edges of the shift meet at the throat, and the collar falls down in an inverted cone. The child's dress is a replica of the mother's, except that the waist is round, and the bodice probably unboned. This pair of figures is taken from a portrait painted in 1626.

By the 1630s another form of dress appears; though basically the same style, or at least in general shape, there are a number of changes in colour. Up till now most gowns were in heavy rich colours, decorated with heavy woven or embroidered design. But in the 1630s quieter and more subtle colours became popular. The gown became a plainer garment, often shown in portraits a pearly grey in colour, and without the buttons down the front of the bodice, a feature of the previous twenty or thirty years. The sleeves became much fuller, and very elaborately stuffed and slashed, and the black surcoat, this time with sleeves, reappeared. The neckline was still the same shape, but the shift no longer covered the bosom. The lace collar became wider, but was allowed to lie flatter, and behind the head; (Fig. 4) shows an example of this style. The surcoat can be seen under the edge of the collar and above the exaggerated and slashed sleeve : its front edges are drawn inward at the waist and then fall away below. The sleeve of the surcoat is split and joined at the elbow, to restrain the sleeve of the dress.

By the 1640s there was a radical change both in materials and in style. The gown lost much of its applied finery, and became a much plainer garment, generally in self colour, and in one piece. In this new style there is no obvious

3. LADY, 1620

division between the bodice and skirt, as marked in previous styles by the pinching in of the surcoat. The bodice was tight and plain, spreading out to a full skirt from a low waist. The neckline was round, and wider than in previous styles, so that the shoulders were left bare. This was sometimes decorated with a fold of material outlining the neckline, and gathered at the bust with a brooch or jewel. The sleeve varied a great deal, sometimes tight and plain with a slight fullness at the shoulder, and at others very full and loose, folded under at the wrist. At the same period the lace collars and cuffs began to disappear. The first indications of this change were a lack of emphasis on the collar ; instead of standing up from the neck it was allowed to fall over the shoulders, and then slowly receded until it became merely a lace edging to the neckline. About the same time the lace disappeared from the wrist, and the sleeve of the undershift only appeared as a small white cuff just visible at the wrist.

This style lasted until the Restoration, with only slight modifications. The bodice remained very tight with a very deep round neck, the fold of material disappeared, and the only relief of this line was a narrow edging of white, as the shift was allowed to appear. At the very end of the period the bodice develops a split down the front, held together with clips. The sleeve becomes much more exaggerated— very wide and sometimes with the cuff looped up by a button, or slashed to reveal the sleeve of the under-dress.

In Scotland one other style was worn, which may have been native, or perhaps not of the nobility. In this the bodice, though in general form as described in the last style discussed, had a low waist which dipped to a point at both the back and the front. The skirt was split from waist to hem at the back and front, and was folded back and tied so that the hem lay along the line of the rear split. This gown was worn over an underskirt. The best extant example of this style is the sundial at Lennoxlove, the standard of which is the figure of a woman.

The styles described are those worn by the fashionable, and then probably only on formal occasions. At home plainer costumes were worn, and plain linens and woollens took the place of the silks and velvets. A letter from the Countess of Sutherland, written in 1616, shows both an interest in fashion and a desire for " sensible " clothes, at least for her daughter. " To my Richt traist freind Johne Hunter, tailzeor and burgess of Edinburgh. 26th Feb. Traist freind, my heartlie commendationes remembred. Ye sall tak the panes to gang to annie (any) merchand within the towne and take off als meikill (as much) blak Ryssillis (a fabric of Lille) as will be ane doublet and skirt unto to me, whilk ye sall mack and furnishe yourselff, and be cairfull ye mack of the newest faissione that is usit. Ye sall adverteiss me with the nixt occazione of the pryces thereof, and I sall send you silver for the samen,——ye sall lykways send me als meckill Perpetuona (hard wearing cloth) as wil be ane gownd to my dochter Elizabethe, whilk, I think, sall be aucht or nyn elns, that be verie fyn, and of an good licht culor, with pesments and buthones sutable therto, with silk : and adverteiss me of the newest fassione, that I may cause mack the samen."

The rich silken gowns were preserved and passed on to children after the wearer's death, being considered to be of sufficient value to feature as individual items in the inventories of " goods and gear " belonging to the deceased.

The inventory of the gear of Lady Montgomery, who died in 1632, lists a number of rich garments in considerable detail. These include, "Ane goun of cloth of gold, laid over with tevell of gold, and sum gold buttonis. with kertill and stammager conforme : ane pink colorit tabbie gown laid over with sylver lace, with kirtill sleives and stammager of the same conforme." In all eight rich gowns, and many other garments, are mentioned. And the will of Dame Margaret Ross about the same date—1633—details " a gowne of flourence setoune in black and orience flowris (orange flowers) layd over with gold leice : ane gowne of orience pan velvet laid over with silver leice : ane petticoat of millan satine ; ane petticoat of greene satine ; 16 ellis of fyne florit satine to be ane gowne : 16 ellis of flourit orience and greine satine to be ane gowne." The total value of these six items is given as £753 6s. 8d. Scots, a considerable sum for those days, even when turned into sterling.

The plainer everyday garments of such ladies were in most cases made of homespun and locally woven material and were made at home, following in some sort the fashion of the richer tailor-made garments. The less wealthy were forced to rely entirely on less expensive materials, even if they were able to purchase them from the merchants in the large towns.

The hair styles of the lady of fashion changed very little during the period. At the beginning of the period it was drawn back evenly, but not tightly, so that the forehead was left bare. The general effect was that of a rather frizzy bob (Fig. 3). The wearing of the ruff and wide collars made it impossible for a long, hanging hair style to be worn. As the collar went out of use so the hair style changed, until at the end of the period the most common to be seen was a simplified form of the style popular after the Restoration. The hair was drawn back tight over the skull, sometimes with a minute fringe, and a mass of ringlets falling down on each side of the face.

During the first half of the period a jewelled snood was worn over the top of the head, often with a feather plume in a jewelled mounting attached (Fig. 3).

For outdoor wear a cloak with or without a hood would be worn by a lady really anxious to be in the London fashion, but most commonly worn was the plaid, the common garment of all classes. At this period we find it being woven in all colours and patterns, some from their description obviously tartan. The material used varied according to taste and might vary from fine silk to heavy woollen. Spalding in his " Memorialls of the Trubles " describes " The ladie Frendracht, dochter to the Erll of Sutherland . . . buskit (clad) in ane white plaid . . ."

The women of the middle classes, the wives of merchants and small landowners, dressed in much the same fashion as the wealthier nobles, but used homespun and linen instead of silks, satins and velvets. However, the poorer classes, the wives of the farm servants and labourers, and the servant girls in houses, had to make do with a much simpler form of attire. Little or no pictorial evidence exists of this period, but from accounts and other documentary evidence some sort of picture can be built up.

As in the previous period, actual money wages were very small indeed, and would only suffice to buy the very cheapest and coarsest of cloths and materials. The major part of any wage was paid in kind. The farm or house servant was largely paid in food, mainly meal, and homespun material ; in some cases the employer undertook to provide a stated amount of clothing, but this was often made up of cast-offs.

The commonest material used was what is generally described as gray cloth, a coarse, locally produced material, costing in 1604 about 14s. Scots the ell, and this was made into a cursory gown worn over a coarse linen undergarment. The universal garment was the plaid, worn at all times, and it seems to have been a mark of respectability to own such a garment. In the Kirk Session Records of Elgin, in 1602, " Issobell Nauchtie accusit for being fra the Kirk pretendit the lack of a plaid."

This garment, which was as much as five ells in length, double width, was worn over the head out of doors, though at least in the kirk it was considered correct to leave the head uncovered and drape the plaid over the shoulders. The Elgin Kirk Session of 1624 records a silent protest of the women of that town against the horrors of Episcopacy, and indicates the method of wearing the plaid. " My lord Bischop publictly from the pulpeit inhibetit the women to hald and wear ther plaids about ther heads so uncumly in the kirk the tyme of sermons, siclyk (also) that they sitt nocht with ther bakis to the pulpeit."

The poor wore shoes only on special occasions, for the cost of leather shoes, low though it was in Scotland, made it impossible for them to be worn continually. Most servant girls and country women only wore them to go to the kirk or if they went to the local burgh on market day or holiday.

Although the plaid was common to men and women, there seems to have been a very strong prejudice to any use of male dress by the female sex. And dressing up, together with dancing in the streets, and irregular church attendance, was frowned upon and in fact punished by that guardian of the country's morals, the Presbyterian Church. " Alexander Smythis dauchter for guysing to be put in the joiggis (pillory)

gif it be prowin that scho wes in manis claythis,"—Elgin Kirk
Session records, 1600. This objection to dressing up was
aimed at the various summer and autumn festivals, of pagan
and Roman Catholic origin, then very common in all parts
of Scotland.

1603–1660 : MEN

THE move of the Court to the south in 1603 had much the
same effect on Scottish male fashion as it did on that of the
female. The English comment of the time, though probably
prejudiced, indicates that the standard of dress in Scotland
was not so lavish as in the south. A ballad of the period,
printed in " Satirical Songs and Poems on Costume,"
mocks the change in costume of James' Scottish followers,
cow-hide shoes changed for ones of Spanish leather decorated
with roses, twelve-penny stockings changed for silk, jerkin
of " northern gray " changed for one of bright hue, and plain
leather belt changed for one of embroidered velvet. The
implication of all the satires of the period is that the
impoverished Scots were battening on the English, and
grasping at well-paid court appointments. Though this is
probably true, we think there was a definite difference in
the costume of the two countries, and prior to the Union of
the Crowns, dress in the north was more sober in colour
and in design.

Although those Scots who remained at the English Court
affected the rich court costumes, the fashion had much less
immediate effect in the north in the case of the men than in

c—4

that of the women. In fact some portraits of Scots nobles who spent long periods in the south depict a much plainer garb than that shown in English nobles' portraits of the same period. The differences, however, are minor and largely superficial. The materials of the Scots are less gay, at any rate at the beginning of the period, and the accessories less lavish. The general shape and cut of the garments are very similar.

At the beginning of the period the top half of the body was clad in a tight doublet, with a low waist which dipped down at the front to a point. The shoulders were padded and squared with epaulettes and the sleeves were narrow, fitted closed to the arm. Below the line of the waist the doublet flared out into a very short skirt about four or five inches long.

The breeches worn with this were vast stuffed garments which reached to the knee, where they were secured with strings or laces. These breeches were so padded, that the figure was bottom heavy, and their width was about one and a half times that of the shoulders. The legs were covered in cloth hose, of silk or less fine material gartered just above or below the knee. Shoes were plain, without laces, and decorated with rosettes. One variation of the doublet occurs, though the effect is the same. A lighter doublet without epaulettes was worn, covered with a sleeveless jacket open down the front ; this outer garment had the epaulettes, giving the figure the broad-shouldered look.

The materials used varied a great deal : the fashionable courtiers wore rich silks and velvets in bright colours richly laced. The portrait of Viscount Stormont, cup-bearer to James VI, in the Scottish National Portrait Gallery, shows an example of the richness of the court dress. The sitter wears a doublet of red, cut close to the body, with tight sleeves and epaulettes made of a series of small flaps. The whole garment is lavishly decorated with gold lace, and a row of gold decorated ball buttons runs down the front. He wears a wheel ruff, and ruffles at the wrist of lace. He also wears five rows of gold chain over his right shoulder. This is, indeed, court dress, and other portraits show the more ordinary and sober dress.

The more ordinary costume was made of plainer woollen cloths, often in black, and though the cut was similar, decoration was much more restrained and consisted of ball buttons down the front and perhaps a belt of leather, either embroidered or with decoration of gold or silver. The noble resident in Scotland purchased material from the local merchants or those in the capital, who sold not only locally woven material but also imported stuffs from both England and overseas. In 1611 the Thane of Cawdor purchased $5\frac{1}{4}$ ells of " Kentschyr claith," to be made into clothes for his son Duncan, probably plain woollen cloth, and in the same year another purchase for his son was " to be your sones claith, with twa pair of hois to every ane thame—— sevin ell of Frenche stennyng." These materials were either made up by the tailor—entries are found in accounts for the making of garments—or else made up at home by the mistress of the house and her maids. For more everyday wear home or locally woven materials were used. This economy of good clothes for special occasions and plainer and coarser garments for everyday, will be noticed as a normal practice right up to the end of the period dealt with in this book. And in the seventeenth century it can be studied by examination of the accounts that are extant. Those of the Thane of Cawdor, published by the Spalding Club, show the purchases of the material for clothes for both the males and females of the family over a long period.

Men's costume changed far less than that of the women, and by the mid-1620s only small changes appear in the portraits. The jacket remained the same, but the breeches became less ostentatious and much shorter, reaching to about six inches above the knee, and being far less in width and bulk than formerly. The hose were long, worn under the breeches, but still held below the knees by long garters, wound round the leg and knotted with a bow. The ruff had also changed ; from a cartwheel sticking out straight from the neck it had been allowed to droop, so that though still the same in appearance when viewed from all sides, it had no obvious opening and achieved the appearance of an inverted cone. Other variations of neckwear were worn, and a flat collar was common. This was starched or wired to stand out behind the head like a fan.

At the beginning of the 1630s both doublet and breeches began to change and grow longer, and a change is also noted in the emphasis put on the various parts of the body. The shoulders, instead of being squared by epaulettes, were unpadded and allowed to slope, and the hips and thighs, so monstrously padded twenty years earlier, became much more natural in line.

Except for the change in shoulder line, the doublet changed little in basic shape except that the skirt became much longer and extended to a foot from the waist. The sleeves achieved a fuller look by having a single slash which extended from shoulder to wrist. The breeches show a much greater change, being allowed to reach to below the knee, the leg tapering from the crutch, so that the attachment to the leg was less obtrusive, and the " plus

4.   GENTLEMAN, 1618

four " effect was lost. In some cases the ends of the trousers were not tied in any way, and were cut to fit the leg. In the next ten years, the trousers in many cases became tubular, reaching to just below the knee.

The ruff by this time was almost completely lost, and a soft collar had taken its place. This was either of lace or plain linen, and was worn in a variety of styles, but almost universally allowed to follow the line of the shoulders.

From the 1630s until the end of this period the change was slight. The doublet lost its peak at the front caused by the dipping waistline, and became a much looser and fuller garment. The lacing and bows which were the normal form of decoration disappeared and the whole tone becomes plainer and sterner. The breeches widened out at the bottom until they were tubular in the 1640s, but by 1660 had, in Scotland, become proper breeches again tied or buckled below the knee.

The greatest change over this last twenty years of the period was in the neckwear and cuffs. Until the early 1640s the wrists were decorated by lace turned back over the doublet sleeve, but about that time they diminished to become a plain band at the sleeve, and finally disappeared, except for a faint ruffle. At the same time the collar made a similar change : it became smaller and plainer, still lying along the shoulders but with an open inverted V in the front showing the top of the doublet. At first the V was unadorned but later a string bow appeared. By the 1650s the collar began to be replaced by a very short cravat, clubbed and tied with a ribbon, or allowed to form a fan tied at the base by a ribbon. It is impossible to say when one took the place of the other, as the two fashions were worn at the same time, and isolated instances of the collar appear well after 1660.

The undergarment worn beneath the doublet was a long white shirt, of linen or perhaps in some cases of silk. This garment was loose in the body with full sleeves. The lace collar or ruff was either attached to or part of this garment, not part of the doublet. A portrait of Sir James Balfour, in the Scottish National Portrait Gallery, shows the sitter without his doublet, and clearly shows the " Vandyck " collar as part of the shirt.

One variation in male dress which sometimes appears in portraits is a long, almost ankle-length, garment not unlike a Geneva gown. This is normally black and trimmed with fur. This may have been some form of official uniform, as more elaborate variations with frogged sleeves appear in portraits of legal dignitaries. On the other hand, it may have been for " comfortable " wear indoors, and is often shown worn in conjunction with a black skull-cap edged with lace, a forerunner of the " negligé " gown and cap of the eighteenth century, and follower of the " nycht-goune " mentioned in the previous chapter.

The normal outdoor garment was the cloak, long and full, varying in material according to use, but generally black or very dark in colour. The hat worn with this was the same as in the south. At the beginning of the century it had a tall narrow crown, either conical or in the shape of an inverted flowerpot. The brim varied in width, but tended to be narrow. This fashion persisted until the Restoration, but mainly with the middle classes. The hat of the fashionable changed more rapidly. The crown became lower with a flat, or sometimes domed top, and the brim became exceedingly wide. Early in the century

jewelled decorations of some elaboration were worn, sometimes with a vertical plume as an additional adornment.
This fashion changed in the middle of the period, when the
jewel became less obtrusive, and the plume was allowed to
run round the edge of the hat.

In England the Puritans favoured the tall crowned hat,
undecorated, in conjunction with plain and more sober
dress, in contrast with the gayer and more extravagant
fashion of the King's supporters. But in Scotland there was,
on the whole, not much such a clear-cut distinction of two
religious and political parties, the quarrel being broadly
between nation and king, not parliament and king. In
the 1630s many nobles opposed the King's attempt to force
Episcopacy on Scotland, but later these same nobles
supported the King when his political authority was
threatened. Thus the fashion, though tempered by a
severe religion, was not in this period strictly divided.

The wear of the wealthier middle classes followed the
fashions of the nobility, though the extremes of decoration
and expensive materials were not used, and the burgess
must have worn garments made from homespuns, or cheaper
imported materials. The number of this class must have
become less as the period progressed, for the long period of
civil war, and the occupation and demands for supplies
made on the various towns, reduced the wealth available
to be spent on clothing.

The average minor merchant and tradesman was
dressed in very different materials from those described
above. The material used was wool of coarse quality and
of sombre colouring. The most commonly described is
" gray claith " of which breeches and doublet were made.
The extravagances of the bolstered breeches was omitted

and the nether garment was a roughly cut object, tied below the knee, not unlike " plus four " trousers. The doublet was much the same as worn by the wealthier classes, but not so tight fitting, and without the shaped waist. It is obvious that the exaggerations of fashionable dress were unsuited to manual work.

Other materials were used, depending on local manufactures, and tartans were even used in making lowland-type costume. As in the case of women servants, wages were paid in kind and cast-off clothing or in garments supplied by the employer. In the latter case, the choice of the material would be the master's, not the servant's. In 1615 the Thane of Cawdor provided " the man that playis the harp " with " Clok and breikis of Kenssir cloth," and " a doublet of fustian " ; these garments were tailor-made. The harper must have been a privileged person, for the ordinary servant had to be content with " gray claith " at 4s. an ell, as opposed to £6 13s. 4d. for the " Kenssir cloth." This was presumably the same cloth as supplied for the Thane's son in the following year (*see supra*, page 43).

The working-class man's stockings, if indeed he wore any, would be made of coarse material, rough and shapeless. His shoes were by comparison cheap, but probably coarse in manufacture. There appear to have been two types of shoes manufactured by the cordinars (shoemakers), for the evidence in a case before the authorities of Elgin distinguishes between " singill soillit (single soled) schoone " and " double soillit schoone." The actual form of these shoes is very hard to ascertain, the few illustrations of the costume of the poorer classes of the first half of the seventeenth century generally consisting of minor figures in engravings or woodcuts. The shoes appear to have been coarse and broad toed, rather higher at the ankle than the modern shoes, and laced or buckled.

The cloak was not worn except by the wealthy, and the normal outdoor garment was the plaid. It is interesting to note that at this period there appears to be no difference made in records between the plaid worn as a garment and the plaid as a bed covering. Andrew Nukill was accused before the Burgh Court of Elgin in 1652 of " thiftuous stealling and concealling of ane pair of whyt plaidis worth 54 shillings money, and certane yron worke, the plaids off ane bed etc." These plaids were of any colour or design, and many designs are mentioned in the Burgh and other records. Blue and green tartan, grey, black and white weaving, and plain white all appear. The black and white was probably a check, similar to what is now known as the shepherd's plaid. Though many mentions of tartan are made, at no time is any name or clan attached to a particular pattern.

The headgear was universally the bonnet, either blue or russet, though the former appears to have been the most favoured. The few depictions of this type of headgear show it to have been in the form of the tam-o'-shanter, with a very considerable overlap, worn flat on the head, with no " cocking " to one side as is in favour with the modern Scots soldier.

Much information can be gathered from the records dealing with supply of the soldiers in the " Army of the Covenant," the Scots army taking part in the Civil War. The ordinary rank and file were apparently clothed no differently from the civilian of the period, except where they were recruited by some noble lord who could afford to equip his own men. There might have been some uniformity in colour where a consignment of garments was provided by one burgh, but apparently they were indistinguishable from civilians, except for their arms. When the Scottish army was in the north of England, Baillie records that a number of English freebooters disguised themselves as Scots, in order to plunder, by wearing blue bonnets ; thus indicating that no sort of uniform as we know it was worn. The only common garment worn, and probably only by the cavalry, was the buffcoat, a knee-length, sleeveless leather coat ; and indication of allegiance was provided by a sash or ribbon worn over the shoulder. Spalding in his " Memorialls of the Trubles " describes the covenanting army of 1639 thus : " all for the most pairt in buffil coats," and " . . . few or none of this haill army wantit ane blew ribbin hung about his crag (neck) doun under his left arm, quhilk thay callit the covenanteris ribbin, becaus the Lord Gordoun, and sum utheris of the Marques (Huntly) bairns and famelie had ane ribbin—of ane reid flesche cullour, whiche thay weir in their hats, and callit it the royall ribbin." Five years later he records that " The Marquess (Huntly) and his followers weir ane blak taffetie about their crag quhilk was ane signe to fight to the death."

The army was supplied with clothing by the towns and, though in some cases arms were provided from the same source, central armouries must have been necessary to keep up the supply. Spalding says that in 1644 " Ilk soldiour wes furnesshit with tua sarkis (shirts), cot (coat), breikis, hoiss and bonet, bandis (neckcloth) and schone." They were armed with sword and musket or sword and pike. Once the army was in England the supply had to be maintained, and the towns were required to supply bulk orders. In 1640 Aberdeen was so commanded. " . . . to mak up befoir the 11th of Oct. instant, thair portioun of 20,000 pair of shois of 10 and 11 insche at the leist, to be send to

Newcastell to Generall Lesleis soldiouris ; and siclike,
the marchandis (merchants) commandit to furnesh thair
pairt of thair clothis and sarkis, being in all, 20,000 soot of
apparell and 20,000 sarkis. And the committe took exact
tryell what gray claith, hardin, bleichit and unbleichit the
marchandis had . . ." There is a rather pathetic footnote
that the resulting dearth of shoes raised the price from 20s.
and 24s. to 30s. and 36s. per pair. Even the cordinars
(shoemakers) did not benefit much, for the official price
paid for the requisitioned shoes was 17s. the pair.

The uniform of the units raised by the nobles is un-
recorded, and though colours may have been introduced
into the clothing the style of the garments would be the same
as the civilians.

The only record of a definite uniform is that of the town
guards, though strictly speaking they were more a decorative or a police than a military force. At the time of
Charles I's coronation in 1633 the Edinburgh town guard
must have been a gay sight. " Thair came ane brave
company of tounes soldiouris, all cled in white satein
doubletis, blak velvot breikis, and silk stokingis with hatis,
fedderis, scarfis, bandis, and the rest correspondent." This
must have been a special uniform provided for the occasion,
for even Edinburgh could not have afforded to maintain
the supply of such an unpractical and costly costume. Elgin
was more practical, when the town officers were equipped
in 1642. " The counsell hes appoyntit the four officeris to
be furnissit be (by) Andro Annand, thesaurer, of ane syid
taillit cott to ilk an of tham with ane pair of breikis and ane
pair of schankis of blew grayis at 24s. the elne at the maist,
and thai ar becom actit to wair (carry) thair halbertis upoun
the calsaye (street)."

The black Geneva gown was the normal dress of the Presbyterian minister when conducting his service, unadorned except for a white collar, and it appears that early in the century even the Bishops wore no sort of vestment. At Charles I's coronation in 1633 vestments were worn by the officiating clergy, an innovation which caused much adverse comment in Scotland. Spalding gives a description of the ceremony and the dress of the bishops. " The Archibishop of Sanctandroiss (St. Andrews), and the bischopis, with white rotchetis (rochets) and white sleives, and hoopis of gold, having blue silk to thair feet." He goes on to describe the costume in detail, the " rotchet, whiche is ane whyte lyning or laune drawin on abone his cot, abone the quhilk his blak goun is put on and his armes throw the goun sleives, and abone his goun sleives is also whyte lyning or laune drawin on, schapin lyke ane sleive. This is the weid of archibischopis, and bischopis, and weiris no surpluce bot churchemen of inferior degrie in tyme of service weiris the samen, whiche is abone thair claithes ane syde lyning cloth over body and armes like to ane sack." Only in areas where there was sympathy for the Episcopal form of church government were the clergy able to wear the surplice, and by 1640 it must have fallen completely out of use.

In the following period, after the Restoration, the use of the surplice was advocated, but with small success, and with the final establishment of the Presbyterian form of church government at the end of the century it disappeared finally from general use for a long period. Indeed it is perhaps doubtful if the post-Restoration bishops used vestments, as the only portrait of Archbishop Sharp extant shows him dressed in a plain black gown and white bands.

1660–1707 : INTRODUCTION

ALTHOUGH the Commonwealth was generally disliked as a period of foreign domination, it was a period of respite from civil war ; and if some of the nobility and landed proprietors suffered from fines and restrictions, the main part of the country was left at peace. The Restoration of Charles in 1660 re-opened the struggle between the Crown and the supporters of the Covenant, but unlike the civil wars of the previous period there was no extensive warfare, and the activities of the main mass of the population were little affected materially. It was a struggle between extremists, and any warfare that did take place was limited in its scope and material effect ; the only parts of the country to suffer to any extent were Ayrshire and the west, which was visited by the Highland Host in 1678, and to a lesser degree parts of the Highlands during and after the Revolution in 1688.

The Government policy was to encourage manufacturers, and by Act of Parliament foreign craftsmen were encouraged to come to this country : exemption from tax for a period and naturalization were offered as inducements. Immigrants did come, including textile workers, thus extending the types of material available. This excellent policy, designed to increase the prosperity of the country, was largely offset by two factors. The first was no fault of the Scots Parliament.

Charles's policy, put into effect by the English Government, resulted in the Dutch War. This frustrated Scots trade to the Low Countries. Scotland had been at peace with that part of Europe for centuries, and while English merchants benefited in part from the war, in that Dutch competition was diminished, the Scots lost one of their main markets. Their attempts to extend their trade to the Orient and the Americas were frustrated by their competitors in the south, who had more influence with the English Government, the prime example being the Darien Scheme. The other factor which had an adverse effect on the material progress of the country was one unfortunate piece of legislation. The first Scottish Parliament after the Restoration voted Charles II an annual income of £40,000 sterling, a vast sum which could be ill afforded by a country almost entirely lacking in capital to sink in trading and manufacturing enterprises. Thus, though there was a definite Government policy of encouraging trade and manufacture, little material progress was made.

This was also the last period when there was a society led by a nobility centred in Scotland. The Scots Parliament was still in existence, and a large proportion of the nobility had Scotland as their main place of residence and, though a number lived in and around the English Court, an aristocratic society did exist. In addition, for a short period, during the office of James, Duke of York as a Royal Commissioner, Edinburgh housed a Vice-Regal Court.

All these factors affected the fashions of the times. The Vice-Regal Court had perhaps the least effect, in that it was a self-contained unit and of short duration, and except for official robes the costume was probably the same as that in vogue in the Court in London.

1660–1707 : WOMEN

IN the period from the Restoration to the Revolution of
1688 there seems to have been a definite division of fashion
amongst the nobility. The evidence of the portraiture of
the period indicates that the members of the court faction
followed the rather extravagant fashions of the English
Court, while those neutral in their opinions or definitely
opposed to the King's policy followed a more severe mode,
modelled on that popular in Commonwealth circles.
This is natural when one considers that the opposition had a
definite puritanical flavour. The morals of the Court were
considered, with some justification perhaps, not to be
compatible with strict puritanism, and apparently dis-
approval extended to the dress of that Court. The
calculated exposure of the bodily charms, as seen in the
portraits of the court beauties, was hardly appropriate to a
lady, however noble or beautiful, of strict puritanical
upbringing, while the frills and extravagances of male dress
in that same Court would not suit the humour of a man who
considered Calvinistic theology a normal topic of conversation and meditation. It is doubtful if any who valued
their membership of the Kirk would dare to wear such
" sinful " costume. The minister of the parish or the
Presbytery would not hesitate to condemn such ungodly
behaviour.

After the Revolution the distinction grows less and less
and by the end of the century, at least in everyday clothes,
portraits show little difference between the fashions of the

English and Scottish nobility. With the exile of the Stuarts the Court had become respectable if not puritanical.

Scotland produced most of the materials for clothing in the way of linens and woollens of varying quality : indeed these were some of the main items of export to England and the Continent.   In the " Description of Both Tounes of Aberdeene," the exports are described thus : " The Commodityes and staple wair which they carie out are for the most pairt salmond, course woolling cloath callit playding, linning cloath, stockines etc."   The finer and more luxurious materials, such as velvets and silks, were still imported, though their production was being introduced into the country. The Burgess Roll of Edinburgh records that Alexander Kirkwood was admitted Burgess in 1688, " in respect that he is well expert in weaving silks."   Thus though home-produced materials were the main source of clothing for the nation, anyone with the means could wear garments of expensive materials.   As a result, there was no very great distinction in fashion or materials used between the nobility and the wealthier middle class.   The greatest difference was between the middle class and the poorer craftsmen and labourers, a great proportion of whom lived in great poverty.

The dress of the lady of quality between the 1660s and early 1670s was that in vogue at the end of the Commonwealth period, though there was a tendency for the bodice to become rather stiffer and straighter in line, giving an overall appearance of the pointed stomachers of the early part of the century.   The bodice, which was either boned or worn over a boned undergarment, tapered to a point well below the real waist at the front and the back, while the " waistline " was above the hips at the sides.   This " undulating " effect tended to throw the skirt outwards.

c—5

5. WIDOW, 1669

The skirt was full, and though no hoops appear to have been worn the portraits show it well filled out with petticoats. In certain instances the skirt was divided back and front, allowing it to be kilted back, and an underskirt slightly longer than the main garment shown at the hem and at the front. Other dresses had no such division, and one must presume that the divided form was used for outdoor wear to facilitate walking. The neckline, which reached almost to the point of the shoulder, dipped in a regular curve to show the division between the breasts, the bust being high, forced up by the stiff bodice. The sleeve, which was narrow at the shoulder, widened to just below the elbow where it ended, and was generally split to show the even fuller sleeve of the underdress or shift.

This form of the gown remained in favour until the 1670s, when variations appear in portraits. The extreme form of the tight stomacher began to disappear, and it became modified to a more natural shape with a rounder and looser waistline, sometimes with a split down the front generally secured by button clips. At the same time the sleeve became more elaborate, being split its full length, the edges held by the same type of lozenge-shaped clips. In other dresses the sleeve remained the inverted cone of the early fashion, but the front was looped up and secured higher up the arm by a button. The inside of the back of the sleeve and the cuff of the shift were exposed at a lower level. This form of cuff was worn right through the period and developed, in the eighteenth century, into the elaborate fan sleeve popular in the middle of the century and so often illustrated in the portraits of Allan Ramsay.

By the 1680s the gown had changed completely in conception. No longer did it have the appearance of two parts, the tight bodice and full skirt, but both halves were merged into one. It became a loose garment with no well-defined waist, loose fitting and following the lines of the body. The sleeve also disappeared and the back of the gown was joined to the front at the shoulders. In extreme cases it was only joined at one shoulder. This made the shift the main garment, the gown being only a sort of over-tunic. This fashion did not remain long in vogue, and it does not occur in portraits of the 1690s.

At this date the gown regained its position as the main garment, and a style was evolved which lasted well into the next century. The bodice was loose, with a low round neck, and a short split down the front, the neckline being decorated by the frill of the undershift. The sleeve returned as a plain inverted cone which reached to the elbow or slightly below, and was sometimes decorated by the looping up of the front edge mentioned above. The skirt was full and reached to the ground, and appears to have been unhooped.

Although the gown had become a loose garment stays were worn underneath. They were probably of canvas or similar material. And from an account of Simon Lovat's rough wooing in 1697 they were fastened by lacing : " Capt. Simon pulled off her Petticoats and sought a knife from Hugh Monro to cut her stays."

The undergarments mentioned throughout this period were the shift and the petticoat. The former garment generally appeared as a white frill more or less following the shape of the gown at neck and sleeve. The evidence of portraits indicates that it was a loose sack-like garment with little in the way of cut. The portraits where the gown is shown as only secured at one shoulder show the shift gathered into natural folds as it approaches the waist.

The form of the petticoat is not so clear, as illustrative material only shows it appearing under the divided skirt at the beginning of the period, or at the hem of the skirt in later portraits.

There is some discrepancy in the evidence of the materials used for the gowns mentioned above. The portrait painters, throughout the period, show their sitters wearing plain colours with little in the way of lacing or decoration. However, the accounts often give a very different picture. In 1672 the Thane of Cawdor was buying " 6 ells floured lemon brocade at £9 the ell " and " 3 ells and ane quarter lemon sarcenet £3 12s." and in 1681 a similar account refers to a richly laced gown. Presumably the portraits show the everyday costume, while the richer materials were used for more formal occasions.

The description of the trousseau of Margaret Scott, daughter of Sir Alexander Hope of Rankeillor, married in 1693, gives some idea of the brilliance achieved. " As to my cloathes, I brot wt me a green and stript floured with cherry and silver mantua (the loose gown) [a] pettycoat trimmed wt a deep silver fringe and galloons (silk ribbon edging), lyned with a cherry tushey (tissue) wt silver. A liomond (lemon) mantua and pettycoat stripped and floured wt silver and lionmond, lyned with a liomond good silk and spotted the mounting fabricade, and mounted with small silver fringes as was the fashion. [She was writing this description a number of years later]. A cherry and green broad stript, as was all the rest, lyned wt a black and whyt damask all through. A pettycoat trimed wt silver fringes, other gowns in abundance conform to my age. Stayes and linens in abundance, and pettycoats and smoke (smock) pettycoats conform to the above. With a suit of handsom riding cloaths mounted wt 6 dozen Beatten silver buttons as was the fashion, being a silk camblet cotton skirt lined wt silk. My own side saddle which I had when a maid. Two stone twice hackled lint."

As in earlier and later periods silks and expensive materials were only worn for " best," and local materials were used for most occasions. In 1676 Cunningham paid £4 6s. 8d. for 26 ells of serge woven for his wife's use, and most ladies even of the noblest families wore linen woven on their estates. Though little or no lace appears in portraits large quantities, to judge from domestic accounts, were used to decorate the shift, the apron worn in the house, and the pinner.

The pinner was a form of headgear common to all classes, and made of linen either plain or decorated with lace. This is described by John Ray, who visited Scotland in 1662. " The women [wear on their heads] only white linen, which hangs down their backs as if a napkin were pinned about them." How this was worn it not absolutely clear ; (Fig. 5) shows a widow wearing a black gauze covering on her head, which may have been a type of pinner. Other illustrative sources show white material drawn back tight over the brow and folded over to tie under the chin. White laced or plain caps were also worn, though probably by the poorer classes.

The hair styles of the period varied a great deal, but they seemed to follow the fashion of those in the south fairly closely. In portraits between the Restoration and the Revolution the style most favoured was that popularized by Queen Catherine. The hair of the crown was drawn back close to the skull, with a high frizzy fringe, and at each side a mass of ringlets hanging down to the shoulders. This style is not universal, of course, and simpler styles were worn. Several portraits show the hair full and waved, parted in the centre and apparently tied at the base of the skull, with one or two ringlets at the back. Later the style simplified even further ; the hair was piled on the top of the head to show the ears, and ended in an unplaited horsetail or group of ringlets.

For outdoor wear the cloak and the plaid were used. The former was more fashionable, and was a long full garment reaching to the gound made with or without a hood. It was generally made of wool and lined with silk or some less expensive material. The hood appears some-times as a separate garment. In 1670 Sir Hugh Campbell requests his doer (agent) in Edinburgh to purchase " 2 or 3 largest quhyt (white) hoods for my wyff." The plaid, as in previous periods, was the universal garment for all classes and varied only in its size and quality of material, from a fine silk shawl to a length of coarse white material similar to flannel. The method of wearing varied little, draped over the head or the shoulders and wrapped round the body or allowed to hang loose. One topographical engraving of the period shows a variation. In this the plaid is draped over the head and is pinned or gathered at the throat, allowed to fall back from the shoulders and is again belted or pinned at the waist, to form a sort of elementary coat and hood in one piece.

The accessories of the period were elaborate. The shoes were of plain fine leather, or with cloth or cloth-covered uppers. They were less expensive than male shoes ; an Edinburgh cordinar John Didhope charged £2 (Scots) for a pair of ladies' " coloured schone " against 48s. for a pair " waxte shone " for men. The exact form of the shoe is diffi-cult to ascertain, no examples of Scottish provenance are known, but they were probably slipper type, i.e. with no lacing and pointed at the toe and decorated with metal buckles.

Stockings were of many materials, but as now finer sorts were much in demand ; one account records that one husband at least remembered to buy his wife two pairs of " peich silk stockings."

Gloves appear many times in domestic accounts, made of many materials, and in some cases elaborate in decoration. The Thane of Cawdor incurred an account which mentions the following types :

> " 1 pair of the best sueit (suede) gloves for my lady
> 1 pair of ruf (rough) greined sueit ditto
> 1 pair floured whyt kid
> 1 pair unfloured whyt kid
> 1 pr. of ruf greined sueit gloves for a women
> 1 pr of treipell whyt kid for a woman
> 1 pr of rich trimmed gloves—for my Lady
> 1 pr of blak and gold trimed gloves."

The middle-class women followed the fashions of the nobility only checked by their lack of means from using luxurious materials. The actual styles would be based on the leaders of fashion, though with the extravagant modes modified. The poorer classes on the other hand were unable to follow the fashions ; the average servant girl or worker's wife was so poor that her clothing consisted of the roughest and cheapest of materials. And in the case of the servants the clothing they wore was part of their wages, which came to them either in the form of material to be made up by themselves or as cast-off clothing from the family who employed them. Thomas Kirke, visiting Scotland in 1679, remarks on the obvious poverty. " The lowland gentry go well enough habited, but the poorer sort go (almost) naked, only an old cloak, or part of their bedcloathes thrown over them."

There is little pictorial evidence to show the form of costume worn, and in the case of women no actual garments have survived. One picture remains to give an idea of the costume of poorer classes. This valuable document is the so-called "Highland Dance" by De Witt, the original of which is in Pennicuik House. This dates from about the middle of this period, and shows figures in both highland and lowland costume dancing in the open air.

The lowland women in the picture show that, in general form, the garments were the same as those of the wealthy at the beginning of the period : a simple gown of coarse material was worn over a shift, the main difference being that the skirt was much shorter and barely reached the ankle. The materials shown are dull in colour and appear to be roughly made. The central figure is a young girl dancing, wearing a tight bodice with a high round neck, which dips to a slight point at the waist : this, though rather higher than was the fashion, shows an attempt to follow the mode. The sleeve, slightly puffed, is cursory and barely covers the turn of the shoulder. The bodice is of dark material, while her skirt, which—though full—follows the line of her legs, is of a lighter material. A narrow apron, almost as long as the skirt is tied at the waist.

She wears a shift, but this only shows at the sleeve and at the hem of her skirt, no ruffle appearing at the neck. The sleeve is full and reaches to just below the elbow where it is gathered to form a frill. The pinner is worn, but in this case it is worn over the head, crossed over, and secured under the chin and tucked in the top of the bodice to cover the bosom. Over this a loose white cap is worn. Three other female figures in the picture are shown wearing a similar combination of headgear, and two wear tartan plaids over their heads, reaching to their knees. One of these is wearing the pinner, just showing under the plaid.

The dancing girl wears dark stockings and rather clumsy, shapeless leather shoes, apparently tied with white laces. This inclusion of shoes is misleading for most women and children of the poorer classes went barefoot except for kirk-going and special occasions, as indeed was the custom for a long time after this. Thomas Morer in 1689 observed that though the menfolk were shod, the ordinary women and children even of the better class went barefoot.

1660–1707 : MEN

PORTRAITS of the male nobles show more variation of dress than their female counterparts, a result perhaps of the wider scope of their activities. The main variation was in the coat, of which, certainly at the beginning of the period, there were three main types. The clothing of the lower half of the body was more or less constant, breeches reaching to below the knee, stockings and shoes or boots. The waist was low, just above the hips, and the breeches were loose fitting, tapering to below the knee, where they were tied, buckled or buttoned. One variation is apparent just after the Restoration, when trousers, untapered, reached to just below the knee. But these appear very rarely in portraits.

The first of the coats was presumably for normal indoor wear, for it was a light garment made of plain silk or light woollen cloth. It was a fitted garment, closely following the

6. NOBLEMAN WEARING ROBES OF THE
ORDER OF THE THISTLE, 1680

line of the body above the waist, and widening below to a
fairly full skirt reaching to the middle of the thigh.   It had
no stiffening or padding, for it is normally shown with a
number of wrinkles on the body.   The edges of the coat
only just met and there was no overlap, indeed some
portraits show the jacket unbuttoned and allowed to hang
open.   The sleeve was narrow and tight fitting, and reached
to half-way between the elbow and wrist.   The shoulders
were entirely free of padding, and the line of the coat is the
line of the body.   When the coat edges were joined they
were secured by button clips, much the same in shape and
design as those worn by women.

The second form of the coat was more robust and
probably for outdoor wear.   It was made of more elaborate
material and in some portraits it appears to be quilted.   The
general design was much the same, but the edges of the coat
met and were buttoned down the front with rows of ball
buttons.   The sleeves reached to the wrist, often with a small
turned-back cuff.   As the period progresses these two forms
of the coat become as one and the only differentiation
between " lounge " and " sports " wear was in the weight
of the cloth.   The quilting disappeared and its place was
taken by thicker velvets and woollens.

The final form of this coat resembled the first jacket
mentioned, except that it was fuller in cut.   The garment
was still collarless, with sloping natural shoulders ;   the
waist was low, and the skirt a little longer and fuller.   The
sleeve was still tight and reached the wrist, but was sometimes
split at the wrist for about four inches and the split decorated
with small buttons.   The front edges still only just met and
though buttons begin to appear at the beginning of the
century, clips were used in most cases.

The materials used were plain in colour, and browns, greys, dark blues and blacks were favoured. From the accounts of the period velvets were worn for best, but fine woollens were also used.

The third fashion of the period does not appear so often in portraits and may have been some form of court dress. A few portraits of the early part of the period show a long, loose unwaisted coat, rather like the negligé coat of the eighteenth century, but not as long, reaching only to the knees or a little below. The sleeves were wide and split at the wrist. This was worn over a tight-fitting garment, reaching to the knees and buttoning up to the neck, an early form of waistcoat. A portrait by Michael Wright of Thomas Sydserff, the Restoration playwright, which is in the Leslie House collection, shows an elaborate example of this form of costume, made of striped material, apparently silk. The coat, which matches the waistcoat, is lined with white silk, and hangs open. There is no collar and the shoulders are unpadded. The sleeve, which is bell-mouthed, is split, and shows a vast shirt sleeve which is gathered with black ribbon to form a frill. The waistcoat is unwaisted and buttoned to the neck. Sydserff wears a sash round his waist from which is suspended a hanger. The cut of the garment suggests that it cannot have been suitable for any very great activity, but the inclusion of a weapon precludes any suggestion that it was informal wear for taking one's ease, as was the negligé coat of the eighteenth century. It is probable that this type of costume was for formal occasions.

The shirt worn beneath all these garments was much fuller than that of modern times. There appears to have been little or no tailoring at the neck and shoulders, the shaping being achieved by a large number of tucks secured by the neckband. The sleeve was very full and gathered at the wrist to form a frill. The shirt was normally of linen, though silk might have been worn by the very wealthy. Though the purchase of material for making these garments features frequently in domestic accounts, the actual manufacture was done at home. Sir John Foulis records that he gave his wife £10 17s. 4d. " to buy holland (fine linen) for halfe shirts to me,"—the half shirt being, one presumes, a short version of the garment. In some cases finer linen sleeves were worn with a coarser shirt, and one account records the purchase of " Holland for my sleeves." Linen was also purchased and use to make drawers.

The use of the broad collar worn over the coat had almost entirely disappeared, and the neckcloth or cravat had taken its place. The cravat was worn in a variety of forms through-out the period, and it is impossible to say what was the fashion at any one point. Generally speaking it developed from a short neat arrangement to a long loose " tie." In the sixties and seventies it was short, and knotted or secured with a ribbon to form a fan about nine inches long. By the 1690s it had become longer and was loosely knotted and its ends allowed to fall loose from the neck, but it was still fairly short. By the turn of the century the ends had become nearly waist length. Until the 1690s lace was popular, but later plain material became fashionable. Variations existed, and sometimes the cravat was wound round the neck and the ends tucked in. Such a cravat is shown in the portrait of a member of the Company of Archers (Fig. 9). This method of wearing the cravat became more popular in the eighteenth century.

The use of the broad collar remained as normal wear with robes, either legal or of the peerage, for the first twenty or thirty years of the period. The collar was in these cases generally made of plain linen, cut very square at the front and about six inches in width. Towards the end of the century, the collar gave way to the cravat and the everyday form of neckwear was worn with robes.

The gentleman's linen played a conspicuous part in the domestic accounts and indeed more seems to have been spent on the husband's wardrobe than on the wife's. John Lauder (later Lord Fountainhall) incurred a large bill when equipping himself with clothes during a visit to London in 1667. " For a suite of cloaths, $4\frac{1}{2}$ yds at 16/-, 3 yds sarge at, 4/6, so much taby. The garniture about the sleives, in garters, shoe strings etc. £1 16s. The making 14/- with the other appartenances in all it stood me some £9 10s." So he writes in his journal. He then lists the cost of his linens. " For 2 laced bands £3 ; for a laced gravate 12/- ; for 4 pair of holland sleives £1 12/- ; for 4 pair of laced cuffes to them £1 1/- ; for silk stockings 12/6 ; for worsted ones 6/-. For Jesmine gloves 2/6 ; for a fusting (fustian) wascoat 5/- ; for 2 whole shirtes 12/- ; 2 pairs of drawers 9/- ; for 3 pairs of shoes 3/- ; For a cloath bag 8/-." The prices here are in sterling not Scots money, and indicate the high cost of good clothing. Prices in Scotland were lower, for William Cunningham of Craigends paid 32/- (Scots) for a cambric cravat in 1675, about 2/8 sterling.

Stockings were of various types : silk, worsted, or linen thread are the most commonly mentioned, worsted and thread being the cheapest and used for everyday wear, silk for special occasions. Sir John Foulis was paying £2 (Scots) for a pair of thread stockings, £3 12s. for worsted, in 1672, but a pair of silk for himself and one for his wife cost him £14 in the same year.

Shoes were locally made, from local material and were either slipper type or lacing, generally decorated with buckles. In comparison with other articles of clothing they were cheap. In 1661 the Thane of Cawdor paid " £4 16s. (Scots) for tua pairs of waxte schone", " £2 for ane pear of sleepers " and " £2 8s. for boutes fiting." These last were probably the soft close-fitting riding boots reaching up over the knee. He also paid at the same time £10 for what are described as " blacke boutes." The great difference in price suggests they were the heavy, stiff dragoon boots, worn for riding or as military costume.

During this period the wig was becoming popular, and in the lists of burgesses of the Scottish burghs we find the periwig maker being mentioned. It was not as common in Scotland as in the south and did not come into general use as early. But by the late 1680s everyone with any interest in fashion was wearing a wig.

Nearly all men possessed weapons of one sort or another ; one of the first actions of the Government when opposition to Charles's church policy was growing was to disarm certain areas. A nobleman going abroad except in the vicinity of his own home carried a sword. These were carried on a broad belt hung over the right shoulder, normally with no securing belt at the waist. Probably plain leather was most usually worn, but some portraits show broad embroidered examples with a heavy decorative fringe.

As with the women there were different types of outdoor garment, those most used by the nobility being the cloak and the buffcoat. The latter is most often seen in portraits in various patterns. The normal type was a plain, sleeveless waistcoat-like garment, with no collar and a long skirt reaching to the knees. The skirt was full, and split at the back, or sometimes at the sides, for riding, and buttoned or laced at the breast. It was generally of leather, and acted as a protection· in time of war. The only actual example which we have seen is of leather nearly a quarter of an inch thick. Some examples in portraits, on the other hand, are obviously of heavy woollen material, more elaborate in design, and a portrait of the Earl of Callender in the Leslie House collection shows such a garment. His coat is a sleeveless garment of woven material, fastened at the front with a long row of ball buttons ; above the shoulder there is an elaborate epaulette decorated with slashing, and incorporated in the garment is a cloak which hangs from below the shoulders. In this case the skirt of the garment is split at the sides. The buffcoats occur in portraits where the sitter has a semi-military rôle, which suggests that it was the costume for active campaigning. Erskine of Carnock records that, when preparing to join Argyll's unfortunate expedition, part of his equipment was a buffcoat. The cloak is usually shown black, and very full, sometimes with a broad collar turned down over the shoulders. Sir John Foulis's account book gives the materials used for a cloak in 1672 : " For $8\frac{1}{2}$ ell stuff to a cloak : for 2 doz $\frac{1}{2}$ cloak buttons." The total cost was £49 14s. 9d. (Scots), including " drink money " for his man who made it.

The lesser nobility and middle classes followed in general form the fashions of the nobility, and the fashions of this period lent themselves to imitations in cheaper materials much better than those of the earlier part of the century. But with the working classes and poorer tradesmen the gap was very great, and the standard of clothing very low. De Witt's " Highland Dance," previously mentioned, is one of the main sources of information about the costume of the poor,

c—6

7A. WORKING-CLASS CLOTHES,　　7B. CLOTHES FOUND IN
　　FOUND IN A BOG NEAR　　　A BOG IN SHETLAND,
　　WICK, 1690–1700　　　　　1690–1700

but perhaps the best examples of this period are the clothes of two men of between 1690–1700, recovered from peat bogs near Wick and in Shetland (Figs. 7 and 8) and now in the National Museum. These garments are made of coarse material, heavy and roughly cut. Though the general form of the fashionable garment has been followed, the garments are much looser, and the " fit " cannot have been exact.

8. CLOTHES FOUND IN A BOG
IN SHETLAND, 1690–1700

The principal male figure in the " Highland Dance "
who is capering with the girl mentioned above, wears
garments very similar to the " bogmen." He is shown in
a dark collarless coat, fitting fairly closely to the upper part
of the body, with a low waist, flaring to a skirt which reaches
to just above the knee. The sleeve reaches only to the elbow
and has a turned-back cuff, apparently decorated with

buttons. His breeches are loose and are gathered to the leg just below the knee, as are those of the man from Wick. The breeches of the Shetland "bogman" are very wide. Their buttons were round and covered with the same material as the coat and stuffed with material. De Witt's dancer wears a white shirt, presumably linen, while in the case of the actual costume the shirt is made of coarse woollen cloth only slightly lighter than the coat. The dancer wears stockings which show the shape of the leg, and thus must have been fairly fine, but those from the bog are woollen.

The common headgear of the poorer classes was still the bonnet, either blue or russet, and showed no change from previous periods ; and the plaid was the universal outdoor garment. However, one figure in De Witt's picture does wear a short cloak reaching to his hips. A traveller visiting Scotland in 1689 described the uses of the plaid : he was talking about the Highlanders but his description shows the versatility of the garment. He states they are not only worn as garments " but were pallets or beds in the night, at such times as they travelled and had not opportunities for better accommodation, and for that reason in campaigns were not unuseful." He goes on to say, " Pladds, about seven or eight yards long, differing in fineness according to the abilities or fancies of the wearer . . . . Many of them have nothing under the garments besides waistcoats and shirts, which descend no lower than the knees, and they so gird them about the middle as to give them the same length as the linen under them, and thereby supply the defect of drawers and breeches." The length here given was probably the length worn by the Highlanders : that of the Lowlanders was shorter, sufficient to go over the shoulders and to hang down to the ground.

9.   OFFICER OF THE ROYAL COMPANY OF ARCHERS, *c.* 1700

The burghs, like private employers, had supplied their employees with clothing for some time, but in the second half of the seventeenth century definite colours appear in the accounts, and one must presume that the clothes had become liveries. The form of the uniform has not come down to us in all cases, but was probably a long coat to about the knees, not unlike the civilian jacket but fuller in the skirt. The official position of the officer was further emphasized by a badge. In 1667 the town officer of Inverness had his " coat and bage of service " taken away from him by the common hangman for " dismeanor," and three years later William Andersone, who held the same position, was similarly punished : " That day also, Wm Andersone, officer, is deposed of his office and ordained to cast off his reid coat."

Definite colours in connection with military uniforms also begin to appear in records at this period. These only apply to the militia, but while during the Civil War the clothing supplied to the troops was the same in colour as that of the civilian, after the Restoration the soldiers' dress was definitely military. A receipt to the town of Inverurie, dated 1672, records payment for clothing a militiaman with " a hat and new blew coat lined with wyt " ; and the records of Inverness show that " Public intimation [was made] that . . . all the militia sogers to bring all ther militia armes and reid coats and deliver the samen to ther respective leaders."

1707–1790 : INTRODUCTION

THE eighteenth century opened with Scotland at a very low ebb economically, after the failure of the Darien scheme and in view of continued English opposition to her attempts to break into overseas markets. Faced with a situation which might easily have led to war, the politicians had to take action, and peace was saved at the expense of pushing a divided country into a union, which very few wanted, with an age-old enemy whose superior strength was only too evident. To crown all, a succession of bad harvests had reduced the country to a nadir of food scarcity, and before the century was half over a rebellion and other minor risings, only missed being a full-scale civil war. As it was, the century saw drastic changes in the way of life of a large portion of the country. Despite all that, looking back, it was a century of almost uninterrupted material progress, and if that progress brought with it problems which had not come to a head by 1790, there is no doubt that the new economic strength of the country had already caused immense changes in the people's attitude to their clothes.

The new materials affected the working class, and the rising middle class, more than mere changes in fashion had done in the past, while the fact that more people than ever before actually had money to spend, meant the rise of a clothing industry to provide for their wants.

The Court had been in the south for over a hundred years, and its influence was no longer of much importance. The Union of the Parliaments meant that the political leaders of the country went back and forwards to London, bringing back with them London fashions, for their wives as well as for themselves. Among these people, as among the artists in all fields and the scholars, a new consciousness of their nationality was keenly felt—and just as keen was their desire to stamp it out and make themselves into good Britons (Englishmen?), in their speech, writing and dress. Their influence took a century or so to permeate Scotland, but it was a stronger influence than that of the much more national legal profession or of the churchmen. The influence of the latter waned in the general exhaustion after the religious struggles of the previous century, and the no less exhausting " schisms in the Kirk of God " of their own time. Besides, the dress of the ministry slowly became stereotyped as the century progressed.

Peace and economic progress, both in agriculture and industry, had far the greatest influence on costume. The home production of linen increased enormously. In less than forty years it quadrupled its value, and by the close of the period it had doubled again. In the last quarter of the century the cotton industry began its phenomenal rise, accompanied by an unprecedented effect on costume, felt just after this period ends. The woollen industry did not keep pace with the others, but the fact that countrywomen in Ayrshire in the 1780s wore Sunday cloaks of English woollen material is sufficient commentary on how times had changed. The old days of self-sufficiency had ended for Scotland.

The greatly improved roads, the increase in trade, both

within the country and with England, and the beginnings
of the movement to the industrial centres, all meant an
increasing knowledge of, and interest in, what other people
wore. At the same time there was the new element in the
shape of the glance to the south for a lead in fashions, as in
other things. Even Jeanie Deans, on her walk to London,
became conscious that she was being laughed at for doing
what was quite natural for her—walking without shoes or
stockings—and changed to conform with the English
custom. People like Home, Boswell and the Hunters were
infinitely more self-conscious and sensitive to what they
found in London.

1707–1790 : WOMEN

THE Union almost coincided with a change in female
fashion, for while the period opens with the ladies wearing
the loose-fitting gowns described in the last section, this
natural shape soon gave place to an artificial one. The line
between shoulder and waist became straight, the gown being
worn over corsets—" stiched stees " an Elgin tailor called
them in 1719—and the hips vanished under ever-widening
hooped skirts. The changing skirt fashions continued until
the 1760s, after which there was a slow return to the natural,
culminating in the classical style of the '90s. It must be
admitted, however, that the evidence of portraits, increasingly
numerous from this time on, does not coincide with that
from written sources. Until 1719, or so, portraits show an
over-dress, with a fairly low, round neck, loose, despite its
being worn over stays, and showing no sign of a hoop. The

opening to below the bust fastened with pairs of buttons or clasps. The edging of the white linen undershift outlined the neck, and the waist was on the hips. About 1725 the neck was V-shaped, either meeting at the point of the V, or wrapping over and held by an ornamented belt. The skirt remained very wide, and the undergarment still showed at neck and sleeves. In the 'thirties appeared the square, low neckline, to the top of the bosom, which remained standard for the rest of the period. Even in two Ramsay portraits at Mellerstain, in which the earlier V-shaped neck is retained, the white frill of the undershift is almost square. Fashion followed the under-, not the over-garment, until by 1760 the neckline was almost completely square. A notable contradiction must be mentioned—the De Nune portrait of Annie Laurie, justly celebrated in song, which shows her wearing a wrap-over gown.

There is reason to believe that the hooped skirt was invented in England ; the number of petticoats needed to hold out the ever-widening skirts became too burdensome, and hoops of osier rods strung together with ribbons took their place. Rachel Baillie had a hoop boned when in London in 1717, and in 1725 an Edinburgh bride had, as part of the outstanding item in her trousseau, " a cherry satin hoop." A writer in the " Scots Magazine " in 1740 advises the reader who would follow London fashions to wear " a hoop of exceeding large size ; a pair of new stays each half year, in which you must lace so strait, that half a yard shall go round your middle." In passing, it may be remarked that a search for the first mention of the almost mythical " 18-inch waist " would be interesting. By the '30s hoops were " constantly worn four and a half yards wide " according to Elizabeth Mure, which is undoubtedly an exaggeration. The shape of the hoop was not, of course, always the same, for it flattened in front and it also divided into two panniers, one on each hip.

Such extravagances did not pass unnoticed by the opposite sex. In 1719 one Robert Kerr published " A Short and True Description of the Great Incumbrances and Damages that City and Country is like to sustain by Women's Girded Tails . . ." Men, he said, were " put to a difficulty how to walk the streets " from " the hazard of breaking their shin bones." " If ye shall meet them in any strait (narrow) stair or entry, you cannot pass them by without being stopped, and called impertinat to boot." Churches will have to be enlarged, seats and desks widened, he goes on, and worst of all, how can we expect ministers to admonish the guilty wearers of these abominations, when their own wives and daughters are among them ?

But gallant Allan Ramsay came to the ladies' defence.

> " If Nelly's hoop be twice as wide
> As her two pretty limbs can stride,
> What then ? Will any man of sense
> Take umbrage or the least offence ?
>
> . . .
>
> . . . leav't to them, and mothers wise
> Who watch their conduct, mien and guise,
> To shape their weeds as fits their case,
> And place their patches as they please."

With the low, square neck went a bodice buttoning down the centre, a development from the earlier split below the neckline. In short, what has become recognized by later ages as the typical eighteenth-century dress had been evolved—an overdress opening down the bodice, and falling away at the waist to expose an underdress or skirt of the same material, or of a different, even a contrasting, colour. This dress, and to a lesser extent the variation consisting of an edge-to-edge dress over a skirt, is the one which has survived in public and private collections throughout the country and, although portraits prove that one-piece gowns were also fashionable, we must trust the material evidence for the popularity of the style from before 1740 to the 1780s. The skirts were often quilted to give extra bulk, particularly the later ones, in diamond shapes or wavy lines, or in patterns. One in the National Museum has an attractive, bold design incorporating thistles and roses. They are slit at the side for about a foot below the waist, and fasten with tapes. There were variations within the style, comprising the shape of the cuffs, the ornament, round, oval and side hoops, the looping up to the waist, and, not least, the tailoring of the back, but it remains a homogeneous, period style, one of the most attractive of all, and well fitted for the brilliant and witty ladies who formed Scottish society at that time.

The Ramsay portraits of the 1750s illustrate many of its features, the Brussels lace with which the neck was covered, the wavy lines of ruched silk ribbon or thread-work on the bodices (particularly the inset pointed stomachers), and the broader strips which outlined the front opening of the gown itself, are all typical. Sometimes the applied silk edgings were stuffed so that they became puffed out and sewn to the dress, almost like a stylized floral trimming. Usually the sleeves were elbow length, and there were two distinct forms of cuff. There was the shaped cuff, a pleated form which outlined the elbow, about six inches wide at the back and narrowing to the front. This type was excellently suited to dresses of stiffer material, brocaded silks rather than satins, and to the woollen homespun dresses in which the country

10. HIGHLAND GIRL
c. 1750
(Inset shows back of
dress)

belles imitated their wealthier town cousins. The tartan
dress illustrated in Fig. 10 has cuffs of this type. The second
cuff, the more pleasing of the two, was fan-shaped, starting
above the elbow and falling gracefully to the middle of the
forearm. It derived from the seventeenth-century cuff,
which had been fastened in front with jewels, and now became
formalized into a fan, loosing its front in the process. The
outer fan was of the material; the under fans were of that
lace which Allan Ramsay so delighted in, and which is
such a feature of his portraits of the late '50s and '60s.

With the loveliest of sleeves went the sack-backed dress,
surely one of the loveliest of gowns. " Sacks are yet admired
for hiding any imperfection of the shape " says a London
writer on fashion quoted in the " Scots Magazine " of 1740,
probably referring to a style in the process of developing
into the true sack-back which fell sheer from the shoulder
to the ground, ending in a train. The heavier brocades
taxed the dressmaker's skill, particularly at the shoulder,
but a floral satin pannier dress with a sack back must have
made a beauty of the 1750s a sight to be remembered.
(see Plate II).

Changes in fashion affected the fabrics used. The
simpler gowns of the early part of the century were usually
of self-coloured silks or velvets, but when these were succeeded
by silk damasks, and brocaded and embroidered silks and
satins, usually with floral patterns, more elaborate tailoring
was called for. In 1722 the Duchess of Gordon sent north
to a friend " sum of the flowered printed satins " which she
had obtained in Holland, and in the same year an Inverness
merchant ordered from London " 26 yeards striped lute
string silk, green and whyte and 26 yeards ditto blew and
whiat making in all 52 yeards. It is for making tuo suits of

Cloaths for tuo young lasses and the price is commonly from 3/- to 3/6 per yeard." By the '60s, when the sack-back was sewn down, and was turning into a form which lasted until well into the nineteenth century (*see* Fig. 10), more delicate blue and pink silks, and quieter floral damasks, were popular. These were often striped with broad and narrow satin panels, or with columns of flowers. It must, of course, be remembered that a bright golden yellow gown worn with a pink underskirt was intended for a reception room lit by the soft glow of oil lamps. As our standards of illumination rise higher, we grow more and more out of touch with the colour values of other days.

Here is a description of Lady Lovat as she appeared to an onlooker after the turn of the century. " When at home (Edinburgh) her dress was a red silk gown, with ruffed cuffs, and sleeves puckered like a gentleman's shirt—a fly cap encircling her head, with a mob cap across it falling down over the cheeks and tied under the chin—her hair dressed and powdered—a double muslin handkerchief round the neck and bosom—lammer (amber) beads—a white lawn apron edged with lace—black stockings with red gushets, and high heeled shoes. As her chair devolved from the head of Blackfriar's Wynd, anyone who saw her sitting in it, would have taken her for a queen in waxwork, pasted up in a glass case."

Until now we have been referring to the world of fashion, but there is ample evidence that many outside the ranks of the nobility were interested in changing fashions. In 1745 Miss Ann Dunbar wrote from Forres to a friend, passing on fashion news from Edinburgh and London. " It was a mistake when I wrote to you no new fashions ; she has severals, all of which I am to have the looking att, and patterns when next we meet. The morning caps are worn extremely full in the border, and full behind. The hair and wiggs still curled. Lady Forres cap, last from Edinburgh, the flowered lawn, the very newest fashion att London. All plain silk night-gowns, worn with different coloured sattins sewed on the breast and sleeves, almost like Miss Brodies' yallow gown, but not pucked. Velvet clokes, laced round with black lace, and made a little longer than they are here, and [? are] newer than capuhins (capuchins)." From all over Scotland orders were sent to Edinburgh and London for fine materials, and as we have seen, it was not only lace that was bought (or smuggled) from abroad. Ramsay of Ochtertyre aptly compares the gentry's dress with their domestic economy. " It was plain and frugal, but upon great occasions they spared no expense." He adds that fashions changed slowly at the beginning of the century (a typically male sigh for the good old days—and to be treated as such) but that by the middle of the century when many changes had taken place, " daughters of gentle-men of four or five thousand merks a year (a merk = 13s. 8d.) thought themselves well off before marriage with a single silk gown, and perhaps by way of reserve, one of their mothers." Ramsay's anecdotes illustrate this characteristic-ally Scots combination of lavish extravagance and extreme parsimony. He says that the seemingly needless expenditure on a daughter's wedding was turned to good account when the clothes were worn by the bride's daughters—pitfalls for the Scottish costume historian—and he caps his remarks with the saying that a country laird's daughters' tocher was usually a ·thing of three parts ; one third was laid out on clothes, one third spent at the wedding, and the remainder paid fifty years later. That the trousseau was indeed

PLATE II

TWO LADIES WEARING SACK-BACK DRESSES C.1760

all-important may be seen from the sums of money, out of all proportion to that previously spent on dress, spent by the Baillie family when a daughter was married. When Lady Susan Cochrane married Lord Strathmore in 1725, she " had a blue and silver rich stuff goun and petecoat ; a blue silk trimmed to the pocket holes with silver net ; and a pale yellow, trimmed with two row of open silver lace, about three nails deep each ; a green satin, trimmed with close and open silver lace, which she had before her marriage : She was married in white ; her fine Brussels lace she got from London ; and she bought a great deal of lace at Edinburgh."

From a tailor's account of 1719, however, we learn that an Elgin laird's daughter was not above having her " silk gown and coat " turned at a cost of thirty shillings, and dyeing clothes was common from the seventeenth century onwards.

No survey would be complete without William Creech's acid comments, in 1785, when fashions were actually simpler than before, and the way was being paved for the excessive simplicity of the French styles of the next decade. In a letter to an Edinburgh newspaper, the bookseller and publisher waxed satirical on the ladies' interest in the world of fashion : " Spinal tenuity and mamillary exuberance (*see* Johnson's Dictionary) have for some time been the fashion with the fair, but a posterior rotundity, or a balance was wanting behind ; and you may now tell the country lasses if they wish to be fashionable, they must resemble two blown bladders tied together at the necks." He refers to the artificial bottom, " the fundamental improvement of modern times." One advantage they had (they were probably made of cork) is illustrated in a story about a lady who fell into the water when a three-knot tide was running—" with

c—7

her bosom frame, gauzes and flounces, she looked, by all
the world like a swan on a cruize in a pond."

Until after the middle of the century, ladies wore their
hair in natural curls and ringlets, dressing it themselves or
having it attended to by their servants. Periwigs were also
fashionable, according to Ramsay and other writers, and the
pomaded and powdered head-dresses of the London Court
were also seen in Scotland. Milliners were unknown at the
beginning of the period, but Edinburgh could boast five or
six by 1750. Yet the pinner, a fine linen (or lace) cap which
hung down the cheeks and could be tied under the chin,
remained popular till that date. Broad straw hats came
with the " country fashions " of the '40s, and, by 1785,
Creech refers to the " Balloon hat " (Lunardi was in
Scotland in 1785), the " Werther bonnet " and the " Robin
Gray." Kay's editor says the Lunardi was for a time
universally fashionable in Scotland. They were made of
gauze or fine muslin, extended on wire, the upper part
representing the balloon. By the end of the period, in fact,
linen headwear survived in the mutches of the old ladies of
both town and country. They had not slid all the way down
social scale, for Raeburn's old ladies wear them, but they had
more or less taken the form in which they had come down to
us as articles of " folk dress."

Underwear throughout the century was of linen, the
finest cambric or lawn, for the upper classes, and harn,
from the coarsest homespun flax, for the lower classes, with
both wearing woollens for warmth, red flannel being popular.
The petticoat or chemise, as noted above, rose to prominence ;
first it was seen outlining the bodice and finally it achieved
a separate existence as the skirt of the two-piece dress, and
the whole front of it was then seen below the waist. Both

11. OLD LADY, 1774

men and women wore straight shapeless shifts ; there is no
evidence to show that the ladies wore any form of drawers.
Stockings were of silk, linen thread, wool and at the end of
the century, of cotton. Lady Lovat's " black with red
gushets," or clocks, have already been noticed. Early in
the century understockings of wool were worn. Mitchell,
the Ayrshire minister, whose descriptions of life in his native
country in the 1780s are invaluable, says that not only
children and servants, but thrifty housewives, would walk to
town barefoot, washing their feet and donning shoes and
stockings at the end of the journey. This love of going
barefoot seems almost to have amounted to a national
characteristic, completely at variance with English ways,
but much more like the French custom. It conflicts with the
recurrent provision of shoes for both male and female
servants as part of their wages, but there are too many
references to the impression it made on English travellers
to omit mention of it. Earlier, in 1689, Thomas Morer, an
Englishman, wrote " Their Ordinary Women go barefoot
especially in the Summer. Yet the Husbands have shooes,
and therein seem unkind in letting their wives bear those
hardships without partaking themselves." Both Adam
Smith and Sir Walter Scott, shrewd observers, comment
on the contrast with English custom, and Lord George
Murray showed a curious anglicization for him when he
wrote to his daughter in 1745, " I recommend you to be
always neat, especially about the feet, for nothing is more
becoming a young person like you than to wear stockings
and shoes." The fine leather shoes of the previous century
gave place to shoes with leather soles and floral silk brocade
uppers, to match the ladies' dresses. Mitchell comments
on the ungraceful, rough strength of country folk's shoes,

but it must be remarked that the damask shoes which have survived, sometimes with pattens or overshoes to protect the wearer on muddy streets, show a high standard of workmanship, which contrasts with the poor finish of the gowns worn with them. The rough way in which the coarse linen bodice linings were sewn to the dresses, and the general lack of neatness in the other sewing of the gowns recalls that tailors were not rated highly in Scotland, while leather had long been available to the Scottish shoemaker and he had a good tradition behind him.

More and better roads, and the busy social intercourse of a century of intellectual ferment, occasioned a great deal of travelling for the ladies, and as coaches were not always available (or to be recommended) riding clothes were important. A grateful Jacobite gave Flora Macdonald " a handsome sute of riding cloathes, with plain mounting, and some fine linen for riding shirts." The fine, but strong, dark green riding jacket and shirt of silk and wool worn by Christian Robertson in 1745 are still in the possession of her descendants, and have been exhibited in recent years. The Countess of Moray wrote from Donnibristle House to an Edinburgh friend in 1762, " I remember, when here, you mentioned about riding cloaths, and I have made inquirie what has the preference amongst the young ladys that are really riders. I find it is a plain cloth with a small rope or twist of gold or silver, for though the white fashion is cool and pretty for summer they soon lose their good looks, and to have as manny as to wash other, which is the way necessary, comes to more expense than the price of the cloath one."

The link between the fashions of all classes in the period was the plaid, which was worn by ladies as their everyday out-of-doors dress at the beginning of the century, although

12. LADY AND GENTLEMAN IN RIDING HABIT, 1785

the mantle or cloak was also popular. The plaids (shawl is perhaps a better word, for it gives the best picture to the reader) were of silk, of wool lined with silk, or merely of wool, depending upon the position of the wearer ; " sometimes [they were] of one colour, scarlet, crimson, etc. but more commonly variegated " according to Ramsay, who goes on to say that, in 1747, nine-tenths of the Edinburgh ladies wore them, especially at church, although silk or velvet cloaks were also fashionable, but that seven or eight years later, the very servant girls were ashamed to be seen in " that ugly antiquated garb." Creech recalls that in 1763 maidservants " dressed decently in blue or red cloaks or in plaids, suitable to their stations ", while by 1783 it was difficult to tell servants from mistresses, a plaint that is repeated by other writers.

Plaids were still being worn in Fife in 1783, however, with the difference that they were " fine and faced with silk " where they had been coarse twenty years earlier. In Ayrshire, on the other hand, although the men wore plaids in the '80s, women wore hooded cloaks, generally made of English duffel, with a " lustrous red " Cardinal (cloak) as their dress for special occasions. There may have been Irish influence here, for the hooded cloak has a long history in Ireland and was recognized as Irish in a contemporary description of the dress worn by Prince Charles Edward Stuart in his disguise as Betty Burke, the Irish servant. His gown was of calico, with a light-coloured quilted petticoat, and a mantle of " dun camlet " (a dull brown material, probably of fine wool, or wool mixed with silk) " made after the Irish fashion with a cap to cover his Royal Highness whole head and face."

Incidentally, on the other occasion when the Prince

wore female garb, as a young lady, he was dressed in
" peeness (pinners ?) gown, hood, mantle, apron, and petticoats." His gown was of stamped linen with a purple sprig,
and there was a proposal that other gowns should be stamped
from a pattern of his, for propaganda purposes.

Presumably servants were no longer dressing in their
mistresses' cast-offs or in clothes bought for them, for by the
'80s in the big towns there were shops the servants could
patronize, and they as well as their mistresses were soon to
follow the current Parisian fashions. In 1707 Lady Grizell
Baillie paid £9 18s. for stuff to her servant Meg Mill's gown,
more than £5 for accessories (including an apron) and
making, and £11 for a plaid. An applicant for a post as
governess in 1720 wanted a gown and coat, or £40 and
gloves and linens as her year's salary.

Mitchell describes the countrywoman's dress of the
1780s as " strong and serviceable rather than fine," and
mainly of drugget, the striped woollen cloth, locally woven,
which had been popular for working costume in Scotland
for a long time and which survived to modern times in, for
instance, the skirts of the Newhaven fishwives. The minister
describes " a short gown fitted closely to the bust or upper
part of the body and commonly called a ' jupp ' ", which was
commonly worn by younger daughters and servants, while
the mistress wore a long gown, also of drugget. The short
gown lasted into the next century among working folk, being
especially prominent in the dress of many Newhaven
fishwives. The simple dress of the young girls in David
Allan's pictures of the 1780s must be mentioned. Their use
of a triangular, folded scarf, or kerchief, is noteworthy.
Usually it was worn with the free ends tucked into the bodice,
and no doubt it could be used as a covering for the head.

It is prominent in his " Highland Dance " and in illustrations
for " The Gentle Shepherd."

1707–1790 : MEN

THE fashion of the last period held sway for a long time, and
the long coat and waistcoat, both collarless, both usually
self-coloured and often of velvet, over velvet breeches
fastening at the knee, lasted virtually unchanged until the
1730s. One feature of the dress of the period, male and
female, must be stressed at the outset, the tailor's insistence
on natural, sloping shoulders. It was well on in the nineteenth century before the padded, square shoulder of today
was born, and the anachronistic disregard of this is probably
the commonest error of the theatrical costumier, and of the
museum curator showing eighteenth-century costume. All
the changes, when they did come, were interdependent,
but it might be claimed that the width of the coat skirts was
the prime factor. They were at their widest about 1730 (at
latest), and it was a rebellion against the innumerable pleats,
which consumed so much cloth, that led to the cut, false
pleats that replaced them. The coat was also shortened, and
the waistcoat perforce crept upwards with it. Wide skirts
demanded a marked waist, so that the upper portion could
be seen to balance the lower ; now the waist could disappear,
and the coat be worn open, or buttoned only at or near the
neck. By the middle '40s the neck-line had widened and
dropped noticeably ; it was but a short step to the coat
which fell away from the neck in a gentle curve and took
the skirts of the coat back with it, until a tailcoat had been
evolved by the end of the period.

The collar also went through several stages. In the late 'teens and 'twenties low collars were fashionable, although more coats without collars appear in portraits. In the '60s again, similar low collars appear, not more than half an inch high, hardly to be dignified with the name of collars. The conversation piece of " The Celebration at Raith ", *circa* 1764, by Zoffany, illustrates this type, along with collarless coats cut low at the neck and turned-over collars. The high-standing collars which came in in the 1770s are curiously absent in portraits, though they are not uncommon in surviving costume of undoubted Scottish provenance. These standing collars, three inches high and more, occur both on silk embroidered coats and on cloth coats, the style thus in a sense bridging the gap between the fashion of the eighteenth and nineteenth centuries. Such elaborate suits must have been mostly for ceremonial and Court dress, and in ordinary life the transition to a turned-down collar with the new cloth coats of the '80s was less dramatic.

Along with the other extravagances of the early coats went enormous cuffs, which covered even the elbows of some coats, on the extremely short sleeves of before 1730. The sleeves soon lengthened, but they remained short enough for the frilled edge of the shirt cuff, of linen or lace, to be seen. In the '50s the cuffs were still eight inches deep, with three or four buttons near their upper edge, and sometimes broader than they were long. They contracted, both in width and depth, in the late '50s to a cuff which was a mere three inches deep, and no wider than the sleeve. There was no need for buttonholes when the coat did not fasten, and the chance was taken to change from small, usually material-covered, buttons to larger, more ornate, metal ones, and finally to the shiny, cut steel buttons of the end of the century.

The cloth-covered buttons were often stuffed with horsehair, as inferior hair was liable to become greasy. Even when the buttonholes were no longer used, they were often made and sewn up again. Decorative edgings of varying thicknesses were a feature of eighteenth-century buttonholes. When the coat had fallen away from the waist there was obviously no need to have buttons below that level and they were discarded. The buttons on the shaped pocket lids (constant almost throughout the period) were more often unused than otherwise, but they remained after the holes had vanished. Creech, satirizing male fashions in Edinburgh in 1785, wrote, " The having half-a-dozen large buttons under the pocket lids might do very well for security in these pick-pocket times, but unfortunately it is not the fashion to have button holes."

Velvet or cloth coats, in various shades of brown, purple, green and dark red predominated until the '40s, usually with waistcoats and breeches of the same material and colour, although black remained popular for breeches. Self-coloured velvets gave place to ribbed and diced velvets of brighter colouring, green and red, or honey-coloured, for instance. By the '50s and '60s, when heavy silk coats were fashionable, usually worn with breeches of the same cloth and with waistcoats of richly embroidered cream silk or satin, the gentlemen of fashion attained a peacock brilliance which even the most daring have not achieved today. The silk manufacturers were given every opportunity to attract with different weaves, never had the dyers so much scope, and the makers of gold and silver wire and lace, of braids, and of sequins, flourished. Chinese embroidered silk was popular for waistcoats.

The fashionable gentlemen did not, of course, dress like

this at home. In the country, and for ordinary town life, they had to be content with sober browns, blues and greys ; and with cheaper and more serviceable materials. As in previous centuries, it was customary, too, for a gentleman to wear a " night-gown," a negligé coat, a long-sleeved, wide, straight garment, usually of silk damask, which may be seen in the portrait of young Sir David Wilkie by Andrew Geddes in the Scottish National Portrait Gallery. "Jupiter" Carlyle described his own portrait (unhappily not extant) as " like a cardinal, it is so gorgeously dressed. It is in a pink damask night gown."

Probably the laird's breeches were of harder wearing material than his coat, even of leather as those of his servants often enough were. In 1713 a young St. Andrews student had his breeches lined with two and a half sheepskins. In 1739 Lord Lovat (Simon, of '45 notoriety) wrote to an Inveresk merchant asking him to see to it that his son was supplied with a coat, waistcoat and breeches of drugget. In fact the good old Scottish custom of making do with what you have was carried to such an extent in Aberdeenshire, the home of fine knitted stockings, that it has been said that a typical mid-century laird wore coat, breeches and stockings all knitted by his wife. Creech, in his comparison of the clothes worn " in a country parish forty miles North East of Edinburgh " (presumably in North Fife), makes the point that by 1783 few men in the parish did not wear suits of English cloth, even the best superfine, whereas only the minister and a Quaker had worn anything but homespun twenty years before.

Middle- and lower-class dress is not usually found in portraits, but an interesting picture by Roderick Chalmers, a Herald painter about whom too little is known, shows the

Freemen of the Edinburgh Trades grouped in front of the Palace of Holyroodhouse in 1721. These men were probably fairly well-to-do master craftsmen with their own businesses, and the picture does not show working-class dress. It is rare enough to have this class of society painted, however, and it may be considered a good guide to the generally accepted styles of that date. The tradesmen include a sievemaker, a wright, a glazier, a cooper, a mason, a bowmaker, a painter, a plumber, an upholsterer, and a slater. They wear either three-cornered hats or caps with wavy-edged, turned-up brims, like military caps. The painter has no hat, and his wig is more clearly seen than the others. Their coats are probably of woollen cloth, dull reds, browns and a blue, but some may be of velvet. They fall into two styles, corresponding to the hats. One is familiar from other portraits, collarless, knee-length, with cuffs which vary in length and width. In one case the buttons are parallel to the sleeve, not along the top as is normal. The mason's coat is collarless, but it is turned back to show faced edges, and his sleeves are so wide that the cuffs do not protrude very much. Those wearing caps, on the other hand, sievemaker, cooper, bowmaker and plumber, have coats without cuffs, their sleeves being gathered at the wrist. This absence of cuffs may be a pointer to working-class costume. At no time have the workers been able to afford extravagances of dress which interfered with their work, and the absurdly deep and broad cuffs would have done so. There is no uniformity about the way in which the coats are buttoned, so that information about waistcoats, cravats and shirts varies in each case. The painter has a sleeved waistcoat and the glazier a Steinkirk cravat, while the mason's cravat has no visible ends. The glazier's short sleeves show how wide his shirt sleeves are, gathered to a band at the wrist. Their stockings are brown, blue or red, and their shoes have flat heels, prominent tongues and fasten with laces, not buckles.

The changes detailed by Creech had not reached the same classes in Ayrshire in the '80s, or Dumfriesshire ten years later. Mitchell tells how men wore " plaids, of thick woollen and home manufacture . . . very plain in its texture." When not in use the plaid was " folded together and hung over one shoulder, and loosely knotted under the other arm, but when used for such protection was thrown loosely over the body so as to cover the whole person and, occasionally to wrap it closely." For a journey on horseback, the rider wore " a great-coat, of very dense texture, of blue or drab colour, either closely buttoned round the body or fitted with a loose and round skirt, which was thrown over the knees and any baggage he might carry behind or before." He comments on how misshapen these garments were—made by a country tailor, who went round the farms accompanied by his apprentice, whose job it was to carry the goose (iron), and the smoothing board. He adds that the tenant farmer and his male servants wore jerkins or coats of homespun wool, " usually shortened in the skirts." Here again we have evidence that the workers wore modified versions of upper-class clothing. Farther south, in 1792, Lettice remarks that at Ecclefechan—" The Scots bonnet and plaid surtout, worn by the men ; the short jacket and petticoat of two different colours, and the square chequed wrapper or cloak, the covering of the more ordinary women, prevailed in the dress of the more elderly people ; the younger person of both sexes shone in a tawdry imitation of their southern neighbours. The man's outward dress, or surtout, is a thick stuff of small-chequed plaid, blue or green on a white ground, and is commonly made in the Lowlands, like a rocquelaur (a short cloak). It is, unless in bad weather, either drawn up round the middle of the body, or hung negligently over the left shoulder with no ungraceful air."

Many portraits of the earlier half of the century show men wearing waistcoats of the same colour as their coats, particularly the self-coloured velvet coats. But often enough the waistcoats contrast with, and are much brighter than, the coats ; usually, but not always, they are self-coloured with wide edgings of gold or silver braid, or of embroidery which is much bolder and brighter than later in the century. Obviously the gentlemen were in the habit of showing much more of the dazzling colours as they walked around than they did when posed for their portraits. The buttons were at first small, and changing fashion decreed which should be done up. Narrow collars appear as early as 1724, and sometimes waistcoats were sleeved. In the '50s metal buttons made their appearance, and silks and satins became more common. The embroidery was in more delicate shades, and the cream silk waistcoats worn with the dark cloth coats of about 1775 had small floral sprigs over most of their front surface, with bolder designs at the edges. By this time the waistcoat had retreated well up the thigh, until the straight bottomed waistcoat of the late '70s reached the hip. This most attractive style is well known from the Nasmyth portrait of Robert Burns in the Scottish National Portrait Gallery. Usually striped, vertical more often than horizontal, they were made of satin or silk (sometimes knitted) and also of cotton. The top buttons were not fastened, and in the double-breasted examples, which made their first appearance at this time, it created the effect of

having lapels, though the waistcoats were often collarless.
The lapelled nineteenth-century waistcoat is their direct des-
cendant—what began as a negligent turning back of the
top edges became an effect created by the tailor.

Until about the 1730s breeches fastened with two buttons
only, one above the other on the front opening of the broad
waistband, as in the previous century. The flap front
presumably began as a narrow cover for the gap under the
waist buttons, when they were no longer covered by the
waistcoat, and gradually broadened to the width of the
pockets in the waistband. By mid-century there were three
fly buttons down the front opening of the waistband, no
continuation of the split below them, but a broad flap
which covered the pockets and fastened to four buttons
along the top of the waistband. This is the type of trouser
fastening, admirably suited for tight-fitting nether garments,
which has only recently gone out of fashion for the " seamen's
rig " of the Royal Navy. Early in the period breeches were
usually of dark material, either the same material as the coat,
or a black figured velvet. The lighter silk suits usually had
breeches of the same material as their coats, but the above-
mentioned portrait of Burns shows the buff-coloured
breeches of the '80s, of which Creech wrote in 1785, " The
buckskin and nankeen underdrapery of the young gentlemen
still continues as if sewed or pasted to the skin." The breeches
fastened with small buckles on the knees, but there were also
small side openings with three buttons.

What impresses modern man most about his eighteenth-
century ancestor's shirts is their number. Grant of Balnespick
laments, in 1772, that " all the night shirts I have is only
twenty and one useless. All the fine shirts is only six."
Seven years later, however, he has thirty-eight, and six of

PLATE III

GENTLEMAN C.1780

them are new. Oliphant of Gask took with him on the
1715 campaign, eighteen fine and three coarse linen shirts,
and three night shirts. The quality of linen worn varied
from the coarse home-grown and homespun harn of the
countryman to the imported fine cambric or lawn of gentlemen, who were not, however, above wearing coarse shirts
with detachable fronts and cuffs of fine linen. In 1745
John Campbell, an Edinburgh banker, paid 30s. for half a
dozen cambric shirts ; the price included the working,
which was doubtless fairly rough and ready, for apart from
the frilled cuffs and the frilled edges of the front opening, the
garments were uniformly shapeless. James Beattie bought,
in 1784, fifty yards of linen (of two qualities, one 2s. 9d.
per yard, the other 3s.) and three of cambric (at 9s. 6d. per
yard), to make fourteen shirts, an average of about $3\frac{3}{4}$
yards per shirt. He paid £1 4s. for their making. As the
coat sleeves lengthened so less of the shirt sleeves and cuffs
were seen. The gathered band of the cuff having disappeared
from the view and only the fine lawn or lace ruffle remaining
visible in English and European portraits has led to the
costumiers' trick of sewing the ruffle inside the sleeve of the
coat. The shirt opening above the waist, frilled on both
edges, stayed constant during the period, but the white
linen neckcloth, tied round the narrow shirt collar or band,
varied considerably at the whim of fashion. A portrait
of 1717 shows it wound fairly tightly round the neck,
with two long starched ends hanging down. Another
a year later shows no ends. One of 1723 shows an
unstarched end tucked through a middle buttonhole
(i.e. a Steinkirk cravat), while another ten years later
shows the cravat tied at the neck. In the '40s again,
the ends could be tucked into the waistcoat buttonholes,

c—8

a portrait of 1749 showing the end of the neckband coming up from behind, over, and down through the third buttonhole from the top. The plain type, wound closely round the neck with no ends visible, appears in portraits throughout the period. The evidence of Scottish portraits is that the lace jabot, sewn to the top of the shirt front so that it would be washed separately, was not popular here. In the late '80s a new cravat style appeared (probably Beau Brummel's in England) which was to be developed in later years, consisting of a bow tied low on the normal wrap-round cravat; Raeburn's portrait of Lt. Col. Lyon (1788) illustrates this. Boys were already wearing, before the end of the period, the wide-collared, open-necked shirts which remained fashionable for them for the first twenty or thirty years of the next century. The small boy in David Allan's picture of the Cathcart family, 1784 (also known as " The First Cricket Match in Scotland "), is wearing such a collar. Mitchell says of the Ayrshire country folk at that time : " The collar of the shirt was frequently left open, or only buttoned and if anything was passed above it, and around the neck of the wearer, it was often a shred of cloth carelessly folded and loosely tied ; for a napkin (cravat) was by no means often used by countrymen, or closely knotted, this adornment being reserved for a market dress, or for the Sabbath's attire, or for some extraordinary occasion." It seems reasonable to suppose that a piece of linen tied round the neck more or less in the manner of the upper-class cravat was the usual wear for working men, if indeed they would fasten their shirts at all. It has been suggested that this was the origin of what was known in France as a solitaire, a silk bow over a plain cambric cravat with a lace jabot beneath.

As in previous periods silk stockings were worn by the

upper classes, while they, and others, also had woollen knitted or worsted for everyday wear. Cotton was also used, growing in importance as the century progressed. Surely the Duke of Argyll's order for half a dozen pairs of goat's hair (poil de chevre) stockings, of different colours of grey, and of scarlet, was unusual. In a letter to Stair, then in Paris (1715), he asked for these to be sent to him, striking a note which has a modern ring, for he stipulates that they be " long enough of the feet and legs." There are references to " Huntly silk stockings " at 7s. 6d. a pair later in the century, and the connoisseur of woollen stockings did not need to go further than Scotland, for Aberdeen and district was famed for its knitted hose. A pair of Aberdeen stockings presented to Marshall Keith about 1750 were valued at five guineas, and in 1760 Bishop Pococke noted that " they make very fine knit stockings of all prices, those that are very large even to five guineas a pair." Compare this with the price of shirts already quoted. As the stockings were said to take six months to knit, the price was not excessive, though most people were content with home knitting at very much less cost. These would also be home dyed, for bright colours were not uncommon among all classes throughout the century.

What might almost be called the national practice of going without shoes when these were not necessary has been commented on in the section dealing with female costume. Buckles continued in fashion throughout the period, though they were on the way out by its end. Their tongues and catches became more complex as time went on, and as cut steel, which lent itself to more elaborate ornamentation at smaller cost than did silver, became more popular, the size of the fastenings increased. The use of steel and other metals at this period is not merely an economy, however, for undoubtedly it was their makers' pride in their mastery of new techniques of metal working that spurred them on to make more elaborate buttons and buckles. The Highlander turned away from the willow bark tanned brogues made from the hides of his own cattle, and sewn with leather thongs, and began to buy his shoes in the south in the degenerate days after the '45. The upper classes continued to wear morocco leather shoes, at 10s. a pair, or calf leather at half the price. Their shoes came higher up the ankles than those of today, the heels of medium height and buckles the only ornament in front. The broad, fan-shaped tongue of the early years of the century became less prominent as time went on. The wealthy remained true to their own shoemakers until well on into the nineteenth century, but the poorer classes were quite accustomed to ready made shoes by the close of the eighteenth century. Pococke records that shoes were made at Dunblane for sale in Glasgow. Burns paid a Mauchline soutar 5s. 9d. for a pair of shoes in 1758. Buckles were uncommon among the poor in the '80s according to Mitchell, leather thongs or latchets being used. In 1785 Creech wrote that " Roses or tufts of black ribbons or strings, tying the shoes, instead of buckles have appeared as a morning dress." The next year, however, he recorded " The most fashionable, large buckles " were being worn. Boots were out of fashion throughout the period, apart from their general use by travellers, but again there are Creech's comments that " The rumpled boot about the ankle, to give air to the calf in the white silk stocking, has still been thought tonish by the few," and " Boots in the forenoon, with persons who have no horses to ride, is thought very fashionable." The quotations refer to Edinburgh in 1785.

The three-cornered hat easily held first place in fashion throughout the period. All who wore hats wore cocked hats. An amusing account of the pursuit, by the women of the town, of an intruded minister at Inverness in 1722 runs : " Under his arm he carried what was then termed a brown polonie, or great coat, a huge wig reached half down his back, while his broad skirted and long flapped coat sorely oppressed and encumbered him, as with his cocked hat in one hand and perspiring at every pore he trotted on." There is, in the National Museum, what was described by Sir Walter Scott as a " trot cosy," a balaclava-like helmet of dark felt, to be worn under the hat for extra warmth when travelling. Much more interesting than the hats themselves is the eighteenth-century development of the old social snobbery associated with the wearing of one, or of a hat as opposed to a bonnet. Early in the century it was most unusual for an Aberdeenshire tenant farmer to wear a hat at all. The following story was told of Sir Alexander Falconer of Glen Farquhar, who died about 1728 : " On one occasion a person from Dee Side called at Glenfarquhar with a view of taking a farm, but having had a hat, which at that time was a thing unusual for a farmer to have, he on his lady asking why he had not invited the person to stay to dinner, told her he would have nothing to do with any but farmers or farmer's sons adding ' Let Soutters be soutter like no hat tenants for me.' " On the other hand, one higher up the social scale wore his hat to prove it, for, writing in 1730, Elizabeth Mure says " Every master was revered by his family, honoured by his tenants, and awful to his domestics . . . He kept his own seat by the fire or at table, with his hat on his head." Hats were almost unknown in Inverness until Duncan Forbes presented one to each Town Councillor.

Previously only the Sheriff, the Provost, and the Minister of
the first charge wore them. The Councillors were very proud of
their new dignity and they created a great sensation. Deacon
Young of the weavers was the first tradesman there to wear
a hat, *circa* 1760. Even in the '80s, according to Mitchell,
" hats of English fabric " were unknown among the lower
classes in rural Ayrshire. In his comparisons of dress in the
Fife parish in 1763 and 1783, however, Creech says that
while in the former year there were only two hats in the
parish, by 1783 few bonnets were worn, and the bonnet-
making trade in the next parish had been given up. The
Statistical Account of 1793 for Laurencekirk in Angus confirms
this, telling the sad story of a hatter from Edinburgh who
came to the parish some eighteen or nineteen years before
with the intention of setting up in business, but was dis-
couraged from proceeding when, at church on Sunday, he
saw only three hats beside his own. " But were he now
here," the Account goes on, " he would hardly see a single
bonnet in the whole congregation."

Throughout the period, of course, the blue bonnet was
the workers' headgear in Highlands and Lowlands alike, and
continued to be so well into the next century in country
districts. A writer on agricultural matters about 1795 says
that in Midlothian, " The old men (i.e. among the farm
labourers) still retain the blue bonnet, especially when they
are in full dress. In the moorlands, where some old farmers
still use this ancient ornament, they wear a black bonnet, to
distinguish them from their servants." Pococke notes in 1760
that " woven Scotch bonnets " were made at Kilmarnock,
and Mitchell describes the headgear of the 1780s—which only
the older men wore, the younger going bareheaded—as " a
woollen cap commonly afterwards called a Kilmarnock coul,

and when they went to Church or Market or Funeral put on a broad blue bonnet prepared generally in the same place." The name " Kilmarnock bonnet " does not actually appear until the next century. Bonnets were either knitted or woven, depending on what the local industry was. Pictures give the impression that the Highlander's bonnet was traditionally smaller than the huge bonnets worn by Lowlanders in Allan's drawings and pictures, and in those by Wilkie, Carse and others. The overhang is so grotesque that one has the impression of caricature when none is intended. The later nineteenth- and twentieth-century " bonnet " of the industrial worker, the peaked cloth cap, is presumably descended from this ancient headgear. Readers may like to observe the progress of a contemporary development, for the informal cap of today has almost lost its peak, so much does the top overhang it, that surely the logical development is for the peak to disappear entirely, to atrophy, and leave us with—a bonnet !

1790–1850 : INTRODUCTION

DURING these sixty years the dominant theme was the industrialization of Scotland. As far as costume was concerned there were more people to be clothed, ample cloth to do the job, and a great increase in the numbers of those employed in making and selling clothes. Beau Brummell was largely responsible for the emphasis men began to place on the cut of their suits, and during the period as suits became drabber, the cutter became more and more important. The ladies were later to develop this attitude to clothes, for their styles until 1820 or so did not demand a strict attention to these details. The old way of giving instructions from a distance to a dressmaker who had your measurements was good enough. For the lower middle classes and below, shops which stocked ready-made clothes were by now in existence in Edinburgh and Glasgow and their advertisements may be read in the newspapers of the time. These shops also aimed in the early years of the century at the great middle class who wanted to make up their own fichus and caps from cambrics and muslins. Ladies of all but the highest class retained an intimate connection with the making of their own clothes during the period and, above all, they were concerned to keep up with the rapid changes in fashion which fashion plates and the supplements in their magazines brought them direct from London and Paris. These fashion notes afford a bewildering selection of what appear to be innumerable new fashions and gadgets. The machine age was well under way ; inventors were to be found everywhere ; and new weaving devices resulting in new cloths were constantly appearing. One suspects also that the shops had not been slow to find that by changing a name you increase the chance of a sale.

1790–1850 : WOMEN

THE contrast between eighteenth-century and early nineteenth-century dress is so marked that the first impression is that a completely new style was evolved in the 1790s. The truth is, of course, that there had been a growing simplicity in female costume after the excesses of hoops and panniers, both with regard to materials and shape. As with the men, the lower orders appear to have moved quicker than their betters, not because they actually did so, but because they had never been so far away from that simplicity which now became the aim of all. The waist of the countrywoman was higher, and the materials she used were simpler, before the end of the last period : David Allan's drawings for " The Gentle Shepherd," executed in 1788, but portraying an earlier period, prove that, as do many of his other drawings of the lower classes.

With the ladies, simpler materials came first. The end of the century saw the phenomenal rise of the cotton industry. In the National Museum there is a printed cotton dress which retains the typical eighteenth-century floral design— printed on the material, not a damask, or embroidered—

and which is eighteenth century in cut, with the back panel
of the bodice continuing into the skirt as that of the tartan
dress in Fig. 10 does. It also has the elbow-cuff and all
the length and fullness of a heavy silk gown ; the skirt is
unfortunately missing.

13. GIRL, 1785

The new style is seen first in children's dress. Little girls in portraits from the 1780s on have white, low-necked, high-waisted dresses, the necks round at first and then square. Their skirts are full, but they fall straight to ankle length. By the '90s the skirts are not so full, the neck is always square, cut below the very short puff sleeves, and the waist is always marked by a coloured sash. In the early years of the century, girls had short, boyish-looking haircuts, and in their simple dresses reaching to the middle of the calf, their white stockings and their low-heeled, slipper-like shoes, they must have enjoyed a freedom which had not been the lot of children for many years. They were to lose that freedom as the century progressed. A portrait of the early teens shows a similar gown, not so low at the neck, but with even shorter, plain sleeves, which could with more justice be called " shoulder-pieces." The skirt remains quite wide. By the middle 'twenties however the shades of the prison-house were gathering. Dresses were still white and high-waisted, but they were shorter, and the era of tubular drawers peeping down below the knees had begun (Fig. 19). Girls' fashions soon caught up with those of their elders, and the Victorian " little lady " was born before Victoria came to the throne. As Sir John Macdonald put it, writing of the early '40s, " Some idea of prudery ordained that their graceful little limbs should be encased in straight up-and-down white trousers, with frills at the ankles, while their little waists were drawn in, and their hair drawn up into hideous little knots, tied with ribbon."

Ladies' fashions went through a similar cycle. First came the light cotton gowns, in the same style as those of silk, and then, when the Classical Revival of the French Revolution had spread to Britain, the white sprigged-muslin

14. THREE YOUNG LADIES, 1798

gowns (also in linen, calico and gingham), high-waisted
and plain, which Raeburn's portraits have made so
familiar. Those of the early years of the century are
surprisingly full. It would seem that the Scottish matron,
at least, continued to wear a few petticoats under her
classical draperies. Common sense tells us that the extremes
of the new fashion reported from France were not followed in
the north, though writers of the time rail against the ladies as
if they were. A gentleman writing to the " Scots Magazine "
(1801) expressed the feelings of many when he wrote :
" Our ladies still hanker after French dresses. Whenever
we see in the newspapers that Madame Talien appeared at
a rout half-naked, our ladies foresooth behove to imitate
her." Much of this criticism must be taken as coming from
old men who could see no good whatsoever in so sharp a
breach with the fashions with which they had grown up,
for although the historian can look back and see the development, there is no doubt that the impact on contemporaries
was sudden enough. There was also the fact that at that
time anything coming out of France was suspect, even in
Scotland, so far had Anglicization already gone in the upper
classes.

Ramsay of Ochtertyre had his comments to make on
this time also (c. 1806), again quoted with the warning given
above : " . . . the scantiness and thinness of the fashionable
ladies' clothing must not be omitted, in consequence of
which they make no scruple of displaying those beauties which
they used either to conceal, or give only a glimpse of."
Then, remembering what he had already written, he admits
that this is not new : " In 1753 it was no less common in
Edinburgh, it being difficult to say whether the ladies'
necks or legs were most exposed to the public eye. It is

however peculiar to the last five or six years to find the fashion
of unveiling hidden beauties, accompanied by wearing very
few or scanty garments, which is no less indecent than
dangerous in a changeable climate conducive to consump-
tion." He blames the fashion on France, chides the ladies
for forgetting that " beauty is never so attractive as when
half withdrawn." And he proves he is a shrewd observer
by forecasting that the next change will be to " large hoops,
manteaux and petticoats of silk or velvet such as were in
high request fifty or sixty years ago."

The ladies had their defenders also, for the " Scots Magazine " writer was answered in the next number by a man who
claimed that he had been a beau himself in his time, but that
now he saw good reason to condemn fashions which com-
pelled ladies to injure their health by wearing stays. He goes
on, " the body is loose and free ; the head simple, neat and
devoid of all superfluous stuffing. . . . I speak only of the
outside," he hastens to add. He commends the fact that the
new dresses have to be washed frequently.

The waist did not reach its highest for some time—
1816 is given as the date in the south—and comments such
as Ramsay's, and such drawings as Kay's (1796) showing a
mother giving suck to her child *underneath* the waist of her
dress, must be taken as the first horrified reaction of the male
sex.

The fashion was essentially one for younger women
(Fig. 14). Kay's Portraits give some idea of how unsuitable it
was on ladies of ampler figure, for example, " Mrs. Smith "
(1795) with her exaggerated train. But one must always
balance these with such a portrait as Raeburn's " Mrs. Scott
Moncrieff ", in which the lady's studiedly artless hair style,
and her good Scots colouring show how becoming the style

could be. When thinking of the older woman, the hat must always be taken into account. Edinburgh has long been famous for its redoubtable old ladies, and one may be forgiven for wondering how their dignity and formidability stood the strain of appearing in public in what were, to all intents and purposes, their nightdresses. Their hats and their shawls supply the answer. Raeburn's "Mrs. Colin Campbell," with her satin-covered, high, black bonnet, with bows, worn over a crimped, white linen cap, is a good example, or his "Mrs. James Campbell," with her high, white cap and red shawl (*see* Fig. 15). Susan Sibbald describes her own grandmother, in 1802 at the age of eighty, as follows : " She had on what it was the fashion for all widows to wear then, a small plain close fitting white cambric cap, with a very narrow border, crimped each side of the face and plain across the forehead, above it a small black silk hood, with a narrow lace border. No hair seen so that it must have been particularly unbecoming."

Raeburn's portraits from the '90s on illustrate the development of the new dress. The fullness, it may be repeated, is prominent in those earlier than 1800. The V-shaped, wrap-over neck sometimes shows the square neck of the petticoat, but after 1800 the bosom is usually filled in to the throat by a white muslin tucker (also known as a habit shirt). Often this ended in a ruff-like collar. His portrait of " Lady Carnegie " (*circa* 1810–11) shows her wearing a tucker of white barred muslin, with a standing ruff, and with a brooch at her throat. Her gown is black, with long sleeves puffed at the shoulders and slashed. There is lace at the cuffs and a ruching round the top of the shoulder and outlining the broad V of the neck.

In the early years of the century both day and evening

15. OLD LADY, 1800

dresses were of muslin, usually white in colour, but light
silks and other materials soon came back, particularly for
evening wear. Out of doors, a pelisse was worn, a coat-like
garment, but lacking lapels and made from a variety of

light and heavy materials. In summer, spencers (short sleeveless jackets) were popular.

Susan Sibbald remarks that fashions did not travel so fast from London to Edinburgh in 1802 as when she was writing, *circa* 1858, and gives as an example her Scots cousin's interest in a dress she wore in the former year. It was a " curricle " dress, " a short open garment showing the petticoat in front which was trimmed in the same way as the dress, with short sleeves, the body open and low, showing an embroidered ' French habit shirt ' now [1858] called a chemisette and a small white chip hat, gypsy shape around which was a wreath of small pink roses." She also describes her distress when, on visiting friends, she contrasted her own magnificence in " a full dress curricle, with bracelets, gold chain, and a half wreath of Lily of the Valley in my hair," with their " neat printed cotton."

Her story recalls Alexander Carse's fine picture " The Arrival of the Country Relations," which must have been painted not so many years later. The scene is a middle-class Edinburgh home in the New Town, and the artist has caught to perfection the contrast between town and country. The fashionable town girl, with her long, white morning dress, square-necked with a high collar, contrasts with the shy country girl, still wearing the triangular kerchief, or small shawl, crossed in front over her dress. Mama is as elegant as her daughter, with a ruff collar, in striking contrast to the wee country body, her white linen cap encircling head and face, and sporting her fine, new, sprigged shawl.

But no conclusions can be drawn from a young lady of considerable wealth (as Miss Sibbald was) travelling each year between London and Scotland, and the stay-at-home

C—9

relatives she met in the neighbourhood of Kelso and Melrose. One suspects that they were much nearer equality in the social than in the economic sense. The brightly coloured French fashion plates were, of course, circulating in Scotland, but the very clothes-conscious young lady probably made a much greater impression on Border society.

We get another glimpse of the relationship between London and Edinburgh fashions in the letters of the Grant sisters, in Edinburgh for the greatest social event of early nineteenth-century Scotland, the visit of King George IV in 1822. The effect of that visit on Highland dress and tartans was great, and will be dealt with, but it is no less interesting to draw conclusions from these letters, from girls similar in age and social position to, and probably not too far apart in wealth from Miss Sibbald twenty years earlier.

The girls describe their visit to an Edinburgh milliner (so the Misses Jollie were described in the Edinburgh Directory of a few years earlier) to select caps to wear when watching the King's ceremonial entry into the city. The anonymous dictator of etiquette had decreed that caps " as gayly decorated as can be " must be worn by spectators at windows. Some of their friends had made their own caps. At the same establishment they each bought " an extremely pretty little hat "—note the phrase " pretty little hat " occurring this early—" of pearl white silk with feathers." They also bought from Miss Jollie " spencers of the same."

Miss Jollie had had an order from one of the girls to make a white satin dress, " but she had quite misunderstood my order. She understood it to be a dress instead of a slip for wearing underneath a robe." But Mary was very patient, and soon worked out how the dress could be used during the other opportunities given by the festivities. No doubt

ordering at a distance made for many such mistakes, and
the customer learned to be forbearing. For their Court
dresses an Edinburgh dressmaker was not good enough,
and the dresses had to be made in London, albeit by a lady
with a good Scots name—Miss Stewart. Her letter advising
the girls that the dresses had been sent off in good time tells
of the trouble she has taken to ensure their safe arrival,
" there are so many things sending down just now that one
cannot depend on when they go [from the London coach
office] unless one goes to see them off." No better comment
could be made on the way in which clothes were expected
to fit at that time than her, "We are very anxious about them,
as we have not got good patterns of either of you." The
feathers are to be put on a becoming distance from the face ;
the hair to be dressed in bows at the back, and the lappets to
be pinned in the middle of the bow, or at the roots of the
feathers. " I have pinned one pair up in a bow ; there may
be one or two bows according to the quantity of hair—if
much, one bow, and one end of the lappet down the back,
and the other in a careless manner coming over one shoulder.
The dress over the white satin petticoat to be first put on,
and then the train to be *hooked in* the lace of the stays, as
that will be quite safe from slipping, and hide the other
fastenings ; the belt of the train to be pinned under the
nosegay, as that will cover the fastenings in front ; the train
to be thrown over the left arm, but, when going into the room
where the King is the Lord-in-Waiting will let the train down.
The black velvet pad that the feathers are fastened on is
to be covered with jewels *well secured* for fear of dropping out.
The gowns are worn very long, but you can manage the
length of skirt as you please, by hooking the train quite to
the length they now are, or higher, if you please." Miss

Stewart also sent ribbon sashes to be worn with the gowns at the balls during the visit, when they would wear the feathers as at court, but without the lappets, " and the rest of the dress without the train."

It may be thought that too much space has been given to the dress of young ladies of a limited class of society for a special occasion. It is rare, however, to be given such minute, practical instructions about the wearing of any type of dress. The truth is, also, that the history of Scottish costume for much of the period covered by this book is the history of the various stages by which the upper classes have capitulated to fashions from south of the border, and of the way in which all other classes have followed them. We know that today, to all intents and purposes, Inverness fashions are, class for class, London fashions, and the influence of Paris and America on both is the same. It is of importance, therefore, to try to give a picture of what the relationship between Edinburgh and London was in 1820. It is only by accumulating as many of these points of contact as possible that we will be able to show the growth of Scottish fashion. The differences between the fashions of the classes in Scotland and England who changed their fashions at reasonable intervals (the date when all classes could be said to do this cannot lie far outside our period) were negligible from the 1820s onwards. It would be the work of a scholar's monograph to discover the details of difference.

Significant changes in style were already well under way by 1820. The waist dropped to a more reasonable level, and by 1825 puffed sleeves were foreshadowing the enormous leg-of-mutton sleeves of the 1830s (Fig. 16). To balance the sleeves, the skirts had become fuller over wide petticoats. By then also, silk had fully regained its place as the principal

16.   TWO YOUNG LADIES, 1830

material for the whole gown ; the silks of the late 'teens and 'twenties tried to imitate the muslins in their light colours and their printing, but stronger colours and heavier materials came back in the '30s. Skirts became so wide and bell-shaped in the next decade that to save the ladies from having to wear so many petticoats, horsehair and other stiffened petticoats were worn ; the old hoops were reintroduced, by the French at any rate, under the new name of crinolines.

The old distinction between Scotland and England as regards the wearing of shoes lasted into the nineteenth century, in the servant class at least. Miss Sibbald and her sister were shocked when they first visited Scotland in 1801 to see that their maids went about without shoes or stockings, and without caps. They hastened to Melrose to supply the deficiencies, only to find that the shop there did not stock them, as there was no demand ! Along with caps, they would have to be ordered from Edinburgh. The servants wore " short petticoats and bedgowns, the latter with short sleeves."

The fishwives from Fisherrow and Newhaven are still familiar figures in Edinburgh going about their business, and their dress is known much further afield from the travels of Fisherwives' Choirs. Here is the description of their costume in the 1830s which accompanies Kay's Portraits. " A cap of cotton or linen, surmounted by a stout napkin tied below the chin, comprises the investiture of the head ; the more showy structures wherewith other females are adorned being inadmissable from the broad belt that supports the " creel," that is, fishbasket, crossing the forehead. A sort of woollen pea-jacket, of vast amplitude of skirt, conceals the upper part of the person, relieved at the throat by a liberal display of handkerchief. The under part of the figure is

invested with a voluminous quantity of petticoat, of sub-
stantial material and gaudy colour, generally yellow with
stripes, so made as to admit of a very free inspection of the
ancles, and worn in such immense numbers, that the mere
mention of them would be enough to make a fine lady faint.
One half of these ample garments is fastened up over the
haunches, puffing out the figure in an unusual and uncouth
manner. White worsted stockings and stout shoes complete
the picture."

The shawls worn by Raeburn's old ladies may have been
imported from India or the East, but it is more than likely
that they were made in Paisley. Both Norwich and Edinburgh
made shawls imitating the Indian patterns before Paisley
began about 1800, but that burgh's long tradition of weaving
soon allowed her to catch and surpass her rivals. The
earliest shawls of silk and wool differed very much from what
is commonly thought to be Paisley type, for they were designed
to be worn with white or light coloured dresses. They were
usually white, either sprigged with a spade design in a quiet
colour, or plain with wide bordered ends. The sprigged
shawls were square, and those with bordered ends oblong,
both much smaller than the large plaid shawls of the 1840s,
which had to cover the wide skirts of the time. Queen
Victoria helped to popularize them by buying several in
1842 ; and the plaid remained in fashion till 1870 when the
vogue for shawls died. The production of cheap, printed
shawls undoubtedly hastened their end. What had become
the typical Paisley pine or cone pattern remained as a
favourite motif in Scotland. In the heyday of the shawl,
which extended beyond our period, it was the custom for a
Scottish bride to be " kirked," that is to attend church the
first Sunday after her wedding, wearing a Paisley shawl.

What the kirking shawl was to a bride, the christening robe of " Ayrshire " lace was to the Scots baby of the nineteenth century. Again the pattern came from abroad, from France. " Ayrshire needlework " is a better name for the sewed muslin, with fine needlepoint fillings, with which the central panel of the christening robes were decorated, for lace is certainly a misnomer. The needlework (" flowering " it was called in Ayrshire) was employed for many purposes besides decorating robes, on the tippets and pelerines of the 1820s, for example. If it had its origin in the baby robe which Lady Mary Montgomerie brought back from France about 1815, the trained workers were available to Mrs. Jamieson of Ayr, because the fashion at the beginning of this period had demanded fancy embroidered muslins, and the West of Scotland was able to supply both the muslin and the women to embroider it. In 1841 Queen Victoria accepted a robe made by Mrs. Jamieson's girls (over a thousand are said to have been in her employ in the 1840s) for her first born, the future King Edward VII. A similar robe, made for Mrs. Jamieson's grandchild, may be seen in the Royal Scottish Museum.

1790–1850 : MEN

THE chronicler of Scottish costume after 1780 or thereabouts is embarrassed by the sudden increase in the amount of material available to him. David Allan's Edinburgh period dates from that year, and his water-colours and etchings began the national tradition of genre painting which gives us so much information about the dress of the lower classes, of vital importance when that of their superiors was merging ever more rapidly with English fashions. In the '80s also began the Raeburn portraits which illustrate how society reacted to the new fashions ; and from about this time there survive in greater quantity family portraits and miniatures by minor artists, and also prints and drawings, notably Kay's " Portraits." Unfortunately the costumes themselves have not lasted so well. A housewife of 1850 was less likely to preserve a navy blue cloth coat of 1800, than a much more exotic velvet coat of twenty-five years earlier, while the thin muslin gowns of 1790–1820 also had a poor survival value because of their material.

By the 1790s suits of silk were worn only at Court, and Ferguson's " guid braid claith " (broad cloth = a fulled woollen cloth), about which he had written as early as 1770, was the material for gentlemen's coats. Great coats, cape-like in their fullness, were popular at the turn of the century, usually with more than one turned-down collar. Coat collars also were at their highest in the '90s. The high turned-over collar appears to stand up straighter in some portraits than in others, in which its front edge curves in a gentle S shape. Probably the stiffness of the material and the shape of the wearer's neck had a lot to do with it. The coat collar was invariably left open. Kay's " Portraits " are particularly valuable because they often show the wearer in profile, so that the way in which the collar sticks out prominently is well displayed. Of course the coat had been falling away from the chest for some time, and by the end of the century, when the tail coat had been achieved, something was needed to counteract the backward thrust of the tails. It was an aggressive age when gentlemen rushed to join the Volunteers and the pouter pigeon silhouette was more suited to it than the easy-going, broad-based, triangular outline of the wide skirted coat of the first half of the eighteenth century. Indeed the dress of the Volunteers had a great deal of influence on civilian dress, and *vice versa ;* even tall hats formed part of certain uniforms. Between 1800 and 1805, however, the collar lost much of its aggressiveness by acquiring lapels. The collar had now to sit at a less acute angle to the shoulder line to allow the lapels to follow the front edge of the coat. The space between collar and lapel was cut in an M shape which is prominent in portraits for at least the first twenty years of the century.

The tail-coat of the early nineteenth century did not curve back as that of the late eighteenth century had done, but was cut square at the natural waist for about three inches on either side of the join and then fell in two broad tails at the back. Beau Brummell, who could probably claim to be the dictator of European fashion, decreed a light or buff-coloured waistcoat also cut square, but the Edinburgh characters portrayed by Kay were not so frightened of colour. Nor were Brummell's pantaloons (close-fitting trousers, often of stockingette, reaching to above the ankles) copied to any great extent in Edinburgh, if Kay is to be trusted. Almost every one of Kay's men of 1800–1810 wears knee-breeches and stockings and buckled shoes. By and large, of course, he was portraying a static, conservative society, dominated by the Church, the Law and the University, which might be expected to resist change. In fact it is on record that a stand was made in early nineteenth-century Edinburgh against the abolition of long-tailed coats, knee-breeches, buckled shoes and wigs. The new " French " fashions (more English than French so far as male costume is concerned) were ridiculed in the

magazines, and one writer declared (" Scots Magazine,"
1801) : " I like to see a gentleman in a laced waistcoat and a
coat which covers his b.....de ; his breeches distinct from his
stockings and a well dressed powdered head. Then at first
sight you could tell what a man was. Now I declare I am
often at a loss to distinguish the master from the groom."
Incidentally, a Kay " Portrait " of an Edinburgh congregation as late as 1785 shows the men wearing wigs. Here
again Edinburgh society must have taken longer than others
to change its fashions, but the wig went out with the century.
Paton, Kay's editor, records that Dr. Hamilton and Ebenezer
Wilson the brass-founder were the last to wear cocked hats,
in the early 1820s.

The cravat was another early victim of change. The
ruffled shirt-front remained as before, with the plain
wrap-round cravat, but just before 1790 the fashion was
introduced of tying the ends in a bow, always low down but
varying in size. Before 1820, the ends of the collar, probably
starched, were seen peeping out from the top of the cravat ;
the shirt now had a larger collar. More of the collar appeared
as time went on, culminating in the choker collar in vogue
in 1850. The style is familiar from portraits of Mr. Gladstone.
Black satin cravats were popular in the '20s ; colours came
into prominence thereafter, until the cravat went out of
fashion at the very end of the period and was replaced by the
necktie. Gentlemen still required large numbers of shirts ;
shirts in museums often bear the owner's name, the date,
and the garment's number in his wardrobe. By about 1830,
or so, such details on undergarments (male and female) were
written in ink and not embroidered.

The bicorne hat made a brief appearance before the end
of the century, but the portrait evidence is that the cocked

hat was popular into the 1800s. Its successor was the beaver, or round, or top hat. Again its beginnings were in the last twenty years of the previous century—*see* Raeburn's portrait of the skating minister, the Rev. Robert Walker, painted in 1784. It is common also in Kay's Portraits of the 1790s. The shape and width of its brim, and its height, varied considerably, and it was not until the '30s. that straight-sided hats became usual. By 1840 men of all classes wore top hats at one time or another. Middle-class children wore them to school ; the clergy, the lawyers, the tradesmen, all wore them. Postmen and policemen wore them. No one of whatsoever class could attend at a funeral without a lum hat. The round, flat bonnet remained the everyday headgear of the lower classes in country districts until well into the century.

The short, often striped, waistcoat of the 1780s remained in use if not in fashion for some forty years, with variations in its collar, standing, turned-over, or collarless. Self-coloured waistcoats, usually light, were also worn early in the nineteenth century, presumably under the influence of the London dandies. Shoes with ties were introduced in the 1790s and soon displaced buckles, apart from formal wear. Another importation from the south was the top boot, of varying types, the famous Wellington boot being one of them.

The male costume of the nineteenth century (and of the twentieth) had evolved by 1830 at the latest, and from that date there appears to have been little significant difference between Scottish fashions and those of England. Sir J. H. A. Macdonald gives this picture of a gentleman of the early 1840s : " A gentleman going out in the evening always buttoned his coat across his chest, and with a great white stock put twice round his neck, and held in fold by a

17.   LADY AND GENTLEMAN, 1846

big pin and a small pin attached together by a chain, or with a shirt front heavily befrilled with crimped edges, he made an excellent suggestion of a pouter pigeon. Above was long hair down to the collar of his coat, and often mutton-chop whiskers, but never a moustache or a beard." (Fig. 17).

By 1830 the coat had completed its journey back from being a tail-coat to something like the modern jacket, in informal dress at least, and the pantaloons had become narrow trousers. Scotland's influence lay rather in material than in style, for tweeds became fashionable for sportswear about that time. Scotsmen of the 1840s wore, as did men in other European countries, brightly coloured, roll collared, ' Berlin ' work waistcoats, made by their wives and sweet-hearts from German paper-patterns. If there were only a few in Edinburgh and Glasgow to adopt every change in London fashions, the significant alterations were speedily followed.

During the earlier periods, small boys, like girls, were dressed as lesser editions of their parents, although there were differences in the eighteenth century. Unfortunately eighteenth-century portraits tend to show children in fancy dress and it is not until the '80s that we can be sure that a distinctive small boy's costume had evolved. Alexander Nasmyth's picture of the Swinton family (1787–8) shows a small boy, with a fringe and long dark curls, wearing a red coat to the middle of his thighs, a short, straight-bottomed waistcoat and calf-length pantaloons, both buff-coloured, and black boots. The shirt style was to reign supreme as a fashion for boys for many years—a wide V-necked, low-cut collar, with a frilled or lace edging. Raeburn's small boys almost invariably have this collar, with tight-fitting short jackets like the Swinton. boy's waistcoat and pantaloons.

18.   THREE BOYS: 1792, 1810 AND 1843

So tight are they at the waist that they look like one garment ; in fact the trousers come over the waistcoat (Figs. 18 and 19).

Lord Cockburn gives the following description of how an Edinburgh boy (such as he was), dressed at the beginning of the century : " Round black velvet hats, a shirt fastened at the neck by a black ribbon, and except on dres days unruffled. A cloth waistcoat, rather large, with two rows of buttons and buttonholes, so that it could be buttoned on either side ; a single breasted jacket, which in due time got a tail and became a coat ; brown corduroy breeches tied at the knees by a showy knot of brown cotton tape ; worsted stockings in winter, blue cotton stockings in summer and white cotton for dress ; clumsy shoes made to be worn on either foot, brass or copper buckles. The coat and waistcoat were always of glaring colours, such as bright blue, grass green, and scarlet. A scarlet waistcoat and a bright green coat were very ton-y." Macdonald thought he was " fairly well treated " because as a boy in the early 1840s he escaped this costume. " Trowsers, jacket and waistcoat, with a peaked cap," he goes on, " made a sensible and neat costume. The only difference in the linen part of the dress from that of today [circa 1914] was that the collar was spread out over the shoulders, and was often pictorially adorned with hunting or racing scenes, portraits of cricketers, or pictures of birds and beasts painted on them."

Not only the children but the working class led the way in adopting the nineteenth-century fashions, while the upper classes held on longer to their eighteenth-century styles. It is interesting to remember that whereas Creech said in 1783 that it was difficult to tell servants from mistresses, the comment twenty years later was that it was difficult to tell the master from the man. The change in the order is

19. BOY AND GIRL, 1827

significant for it is not too much to say that the masters were, by 1800, adopting new fashions which their servants had already taken up, or were quicker to do so. It was a levelling upwards of fashion, not down as previously. Fashionable eighteenth-century dress was not suitable for a working man, particularly not for a worker at a machine, and what authentic representations we have demonstrate that the worker had to adapt the style fairly drastically. The worker had to wear a short, hip-length coat long before the man of fashion—*see* David Allan's drawings for " The Gentle Shepherd " in 1788, but specifically stated to represent an earlier period. The new fashions, however, were much more suitable, and homespun materials were easily adapted to them, while the revolution in the spinning and weaving industries soon brought factory-made woollen clothes within the reach of most, if not all, workers.

The dress of a Borderer, a coachman at the big house, is worth quoting from Susan Sibbald's " Memoirs " 1802 : " David's Sabbath day's ' shute ' was, his coat (with large white buttons) of Galashiels blue (which is of a lighter shade than Waterloo blue), his waistcoat and Small clothes [breeches] of the same, iron grey worsted stockings, very broad-toed shoes, and brass buckles, a gay coloured handkerchief about his neck, and a rather flat crowned hat."

To take but one example of how the lower classes were in advance of their " betters " in the nineteenth century, attention is drawn to the figure of Adam Fergusson in Sir David Wilkie's picture of Sir Walter Scott's family " in the garb of rustic peasants " (1815)—his coat does not fall away in tails but is cut almost straight down from the waist as was the fashion many years later. Again, in John Ainslie's picture of " The Servants at Dalkeith House " in 1832, the mail

20.   WORKING-CLASS MAN AND WOMAN, 1832

carrier wears trousers with legs about the same width as had recently become fashionable in London, not because he followed fashion but because, for practical reasons, he was in advance of it (Fig. 20). Even in 1840 the wearing of trousers is noted as being only " practically universal " and these were extremely narrow, " strapped down over boots during the day, and over shoes at night." Coat sleeves were as tight as the trousers.

An observer of the dress of the farming community in the middle '90s comments : " Their clothing partakes of the improvement which has taken place in the different branches of that manufacture ; being for the most part bought in Edinburgh, where is to be had great variety of stuff suitable to their circumstances, cheap and strong, also decent and becoming." He goes on to describe the Sunday dress of a young ploughman as follows, " a coat of blue cloth, at 5/6 the yard ; velveret [sic] vest corduroy breeches, white cotton stockings, calf-skin shoes with black silk shoe-knots, shirt with ruffles at the breast and a white muslin fringed cravat, hat worth 8s. or 10s. The shoe-knots and ruffles are indeed rather uncommon, but all the other articles are very much in use."

The evidence from the other counties points in the same direction, that Robert Burns' obvious concern for his dress was shared by others of his class, and was in no way connected with the vanity of genius. The young Aberdeenshire farmer of the early nineteenth century, for instance, had " at least, one suit of good English cloth," however plainly he dressed when at work. Indeed it was often the case that " those who dress most genteely at church or market, are most indefatigable and active in conducting the plough or cart, or weilding the hoe and scythe." The usual dress of

PLATE IV

A COUNTRY FAMILY, EARLY NINETEENTH CENTURY

Angus ploughmen about 1810 was " a grey felt, or straw, or glazed hat ; a short drab coat, striped waistcoat, with white or blue pantaloons or trousers." When they went to the kirk, however, they dressed " in English clothes " and could " hardly be distinguished from their masters."

This is perhaps the most fitting end that a survey of Scottish costume could have, with its references both to the democratization and the anglicization of our fashions.

WEAPONS

THE weapons, offensive and defensive, used in Scotland throughout the three hundred years under review were, by and large, the same as those used by the other nations of Europe. The story that some Highlanders enlisted under Prince Charles Edward's banner carrying scythes and bill-hooks does not mean that Scotland lagged behind in adopting new weapons, but is rather a tribute to the settled state of this so-called backward area. Throughout the period war became more and more an organized pastime, and, as always happens, the gap between professionals and amateurs widened. Scottish armies always had a nucleus of professionals available, men trained in the foreign wars of France, the Thirty Years' War and the campaigns in the Low Countries, and they, like the Scottish knights of the Middle Ages, were equipped in exactly the same manner as other professional soldiers throughout Europe. The weapons to be described, therefore, are the particularly Scottish (usually Highland) versions of those weapons, which the professionals and their amateur comrades used when at home and fighting under Scottish conditions.

When the barons and lairds of the Borders were commanded to meet the Governor of Scotland (Arran) with their followers at Jedburgh on 27th October 1552 " bodin in feyre of weyre " (equipped for warfare), to make an example of the Kerrs after their murder of Sir Walter Scott of Buccleugh in the High Street of Edinburgh, they would be expected to wear bonnets and body armour of steel (if they had them ; failing that, jacks or leather doublets) and to be armed with swords, single (or two-handed among the craftsmen), spears, and versions of the European pole weapon. The spear was probably what was known as the " Jeddart stave," and the pole weapon a " Lochaber axe," but precise descriptions of what these were defy enquiry. Possession of firearms would be confined to the wealthier members of the muster and the " hakbutaris," who, being professionals, were on such occasions paid and supplied by the central government. Hagbuts were hand cannons, some three feet in length. The cannon needed on this occasion were also supplied by the Governor. Mons Meg, the great siege gun of 20 inches calibre still to be seen in Edinburgh Castle, was a century old by this time and was not required for a mere punitive expedition. She was still able to fire up to a range of two miles, as was proved when she was discharged during the celebrations following the young Queen Mary's marriage to the Dauphin of France in 1558. Four falcons, small siege guns drawn by horses and plentifully supplied with powder and iron shot, were sent down with the party.

The manufacture of hand firearms began in Scotland in the second half of the sixteenth century, the earliest dated pistols being from the last decade. The peculiarity of the Scottish pistol from then until after the '45 Rebellion, when the craft was in decline, lies in the fact that the weapon was made entirely from metal. In England and throughout Europe metal gave place to wood for the stock and butt, yet in Scotland, though wooden stocks and butts are found, pistol-making died as it began, a metal workers' craft. The reason was the innate conservatism of the Highland area of the country. As with their dress, so with their weapons, the Highlanders, having accepted a new idea or fashion, retained it long after everyone else had discarded it, adapted it to suit their own conditions, and imposed their own artistic heritage on it. The early pistols, with snaphaunce locks (distinguished from the later flintlocks by the way in which the steel against which the flint strikes was made separately from the priming pan ; the snaphaunce could not be set at half-cock as could the later pistol) were made on the east coast and no doubt were supplied to customers in all parts. One pair of brass pistols with early fish-tail butts (the flat butt bifurcates, one terminal like that of a fish's tail, the other rounded) was made for Louis XIII of France by John Low of Dundee in 1611. This historic pair found their way to Russia after the French Revolution, and returned to this country after the Russian Revolution. They now form part of the Whitelaw collection in the National Museum. Another early type has a lemon or globose-shaped butt, a form common to the European wheellock pistols of the sixteenth and seventeenth centuries. Both types often bear the maker's initials on the lock plate. The third variety, with its origin in the first half of the seventeenth century, has a heart-shaped butt, yet another example of Scottish interest in the heart as an artistic form. These are usually of steel, though one pistol in the National Museum, with claims to being considered the finest of all, has a rosewood butt. The brasswork of the earlier types lent itself to engraving, mostly floral and leaf designs and scrolls of Renaissance origin, with nothing particularly Scottish about them. The steel heart butts usually have inlaid silver decoration, often heart shapes, but the next type, the scroll or ram's horn butt, also made of steel, has engraved decoration as well as silver, and even gold, inlays. The flat butt of this type ends in two inward-turning scrolls, with the silver ball-ended pricker (for cleaning the lock) between them. The trigger is also silver and ball-shaped (*see* Fig. 21A). Late seventeenth- and early eighteenth-century scroll butts, it should be added, are decorated more in the manner of the heart butts.

21A. SCROLL-BUTT HIGHLAND PISTOL OF
     STEEL, FIRST HALF OF THE EIGHTEENTH
     CENTURY

21B. HIGHLAND POWDER HORN, *c.* 1700

It is the eighteenth-century flintlock scroll butt pistol which may be considered the Highland pistol *par excellence*. Made in a number of villages along the Highland line, with

Doune holding first place, for the Highland market at a
time when the Lowlands had succumbed to the English and
Continental wooden-butted types, these pistols were the
work of men who deserve as few have deserved the name of
artist-craftsmen. The Caddells, Campbells, Murdochs and
Christies produced weapons whose efficiency was a tribute
to their craftsmanship, and whose artistry is evident to all.
Yet their profuse engraving owes nothing to Celtic art forms,
being Renaissance in origin, with touches of eighteenth-
century classicism. It must be remembered that by the
second quarter of the eighteenth century the round brooches
and the powder horns had lost much of the spirit of their
Celtic decoration, and that in any case there was no tradition
in pistol decoration such as the brooches and horns had
possessed.

In the eighteenth century steel pistols were made with
butts like the contemporary European pistol, usually
described as love-shaped. These were the work of the same
craftsmen as the others, and they are just as efficient as
weapons while lacking the beauty of the scroll butts.

Scottish pistols were always made in pairs and, until
about 1700, with right- and left-handed locks. They have
long belt-hooks for clipping over the waist-belt, for they were
not carried in holsters. A final peculiarity is that, one and
all, they lack trigger guards and sights. The acuteness of
the curve of the butt is one way of telling the age of a pistol,
for the line of butt and barrel is much straighter in earlier
examples.

After 1775 at latest, the great tradition had gone and the
great names are heard no more. The Highland regiments
were supplied from Birmingham with a steel pistol which
was a travesty of the real thing, and there was no longer any

need for a private individual to carry pistols about with him, or possess them in case he was suddenly called upon to be a soldier. Only with the nineteenth-century Highland dress revival did the pistols come into civilian life again, and then merely as costume accessories. No doubt the pistols which one of his would-be Highland subjects dropped on George IV's toe at a Holyrood levee was a London-made, costume-pistol. The Clanranald pistols, with their enamelled butt plates, now in the National Museum, are of this vintage. In their way they are fine enough, but if placed beside the earlier pistols, the full extent of the deception is seen.

During the seventeenth century a distinctive musket was made for use in the Highlands, with a lock mechanism similar to that of the pistols and easily known by their fluted, curving butts (see Plate I).

Generally speaking, the sword used during the period was that used in England. There is, so far as is known, no Scottish variety of the small sword, the narrow bladed weapon, with a knuckle bow hilt guard and shrunken quillons, which was the civilian's weapon in both countries in the seventeenth and eighteenth centuries. There are, however, important Scottish characteristics both in the two-handed sword and in the basket-hilted sword, although as types they are European. The two-hander probably came to Scotland just before 1500 and lasted till about 1650, or later as an archaic weapon in the Highlands. The form was European, but there were three Scottish types. First there was the sword with a plain cross-guard and two ring-shaped guards, one each side at right angles to the quillons (the cross-guards). Some of these are very large and are ceremonial swords. A sword with plain, straight quillons, round in cross-section, which drop at the ends, has two iron shells attached at the quillons and projecting up the hilt to protect the hands. This was later in date, probably late sixteenth century, and of native origin. Finally, but earlier than the shell-guard sword, there is what is considered the typical Scottish claymore (from the Gaelic = the big sword), a beautifully proportioned, two-handed weapon, about 3 feet 6 inches in length, with downward drooping quillons which end in pierced quatrefoils, and having a round disc pommel. The word " claymore " was used in the eighteenth century in contexts which prove that the basket-hilted broadsword is meant. This usage has been continued by the Army, but no student of weapons should fail to distinguish them, by calling the two-hander the claymore, and the other the basket-hilted broadsword.

When armour went out of fashion, the steel glove covering the sword hand went with it, and protection for the hand had to be transferred to the sword itself. Probably derived from a German prototype, there was evolved in Britain a single-handed sword in which the hand was protected by a steel basket. In the seventeenth century the weapon was used in both Lowlands and Highlands, and at least one variety was common to Scotland and England— the Mortuary hilted sword. In the eighteenth century it became a cavalry weapon in the south and remained a foot-soldier's sword in the Highlands. The broadsword is a " general purposes " weapon, for fencing and for the cut and thrust of a charge on horse or afoot. The backsword, with a single-edged blade, is a more delicate weapon, usually with a narrower blade ; it also was common in Scotland.

Sword blades were made in Scotland, but they cannot now be positively identified. The majority of seventeenth- and eighteenth-century weapons had blades which were forged in Germany ; others came from Holland and Spain, and even from England, though an Englishman, Thomas Morer, writing about 1689, admitted that the Highlanders had " the best blades now in being." Because of that, he adds, they were much sought after by the English officers and men, who were well supplied with them before leaving the country. Many English broadsword blades were made at Shotley Bridge in Northumberland. Hilts were made in Scotland, but their makers' names are not known from signatures until the end of the seventeenth century. Armourers' names are, of course, to be found in records ; they were members of the Hammermen's Guild. The earliest hilts, both types confined to the seventeenth century, are not beautiful, consisting either of broad, flat, iron ribbons welded together, or narrower bars which broaden where the counter-guards cross. A basket-hilt may be considered as consisting of a main guard curving from the blade to the pommel, and subsidiary guards, opposite each other, and at right angles (more or less) to the plane of the main guard. The counter-guards run diagonally between the main and subsidiary guards. From the early forms there evolved the pierced basket hilt, in which the enlarged junction plate (the meeting of the counter-guards) is fretted and pierced with hearts and circles. There are variations within the type ; the bars are sometimes fluted, or decorated with dot and circle ornament and sometimes the entire hilt was made of brass, but the pierced hilt became the standard model, and was the pattern for Army swords. Examples with oval holes on the inside of the hilt are cavalry swords, the rider being enabled to hold the reins with his thumb. The sword makers of Glasgow and Stirling were not content to be tied to one form, and in the early years of the eighteenth century they put all their skill into what are considered the finest examples, each one a work of art made by men so confident of their material and their own skill that they could take liberties with their designs and still produce first-class weapons. And so pleased were they with the results that they signed the hilts with their initials and the first letter of the town in which they were made. Walter and John Allan of Stirling and the Simpsons and Thomas Gemmill of Glasgow and Gorbals, can take their place beside the great pistol makers as artist-craftsmen. In their hilts, diamond shapes, curving bars, even thistles take the place of the standard design. Some are inlaid with silver and, very rarely, with gold. A few silver hilts were also made in Scotland ; though graceful, they are essentially silversmiths' work and not in the real tradition.

Many blades bear the name of Andrea Ferarra, variously spelled. Why the name of an Italian swordsmith of the mid-sixteenth century should have been necessary to convince hard-headed seventeenth- and eighteenth-century Scots that a blade was a good one is a mystery. Certainly the blades so marked have less connection with Ferarra than has a modern golf club with the tournament professional whose name it bears. A number of blades have etched and gilded decoration near the hilt. That these were made in Germany for the Scottish market is proved by their inscriptions— " God protect the upright Scots " (in German), " Prosperity for Schotland and No Union," and " God bless King James the Eighth." A close relation of the basket hilt was the Mortuary hilted sword, which has a male head in low relief on the underside of the broadened main guard, probably intended at first as a portrait of Charles I. Seventeenth-century scabbards were made from two thin laths of wood covered with leather, the surface of which was tooled with small devices ; a brass chape and iron hook were the only mountings. The hook was for attaching the sword to the cross- or waist-belt. Later scabbards were made entirely from leather, and had steel or silver shapes and lockets.

The dagger used in Scotland in the late sixteenth century was the same as that used in other countries, but there appears to have been some preference for a wooden-hilted, silver-mounted dagger, with a fretted grip, which narrowed as it approached the blade before swelling into haunches. Below these and resting on the blade was a crescent-shaped mount of iron. The ever-conservative Highlander probably derived his seventeenth- and eighteenth-century dirk from this variety, after daggers had gone out of fashion in other countries. The Highland dirk was a stabbing weapon for close fighting (and also for many unwarlike purposes) with a characteristic pommel and a blade triangular in cross-section, with a thick back edge. Seventeenth-century dirks have small hilts with wide, flat-topped pommels. There are usually two bands of Celtic interlacing ornament on the grip. As time went on, the carving expanded until it covered the whole grip. It also became deeper and was studded with brass nails. The brass (sometimes pewter) pommel plate was at times pierced or engraved with heart or other shapes. Whether the hilt was of wood or, as in some cases of brass or horn, the shape remained the same until after the '45. The later eighteenth- and early nineteenth-century dirk was either mass-produced for Army issue or a costumier's weapon, an essential part of " Highland Costume." The carving deteriorated in spirit, the hilt became baluster-shaped, in deference to eighteenth-century classicism but with no thought to the shape of the hand which wielded it. As a final indignity, pommels were mounted with cairngorms,

or other semi-precious stones, or polished pebbles. The
pommel was even tilted forward to allow the mounts to be
seen. Blades also deteriorated ; previously they were often
sword blades cut down. Dirk sheaths, sometimes with holes
to take a knife and fork, were of leather, thonged down the
back and the surface tooled with repeating patterns.

Another vehicle for the Highlander's art—the dirk is
purely Highland, its decoration in the Celtic tradition—and
his skill in leatherwork, was the Targe or shield. To quote
Morer again : " When they are on the Defensive Part, they
depend much on Targes or Targets . . . which are shields
of that form the Latines call by the Name of Clypeus, round
and aequidistant from the center ; And are made from the
toughest Wood they can get, lined within and covered
without with Skins, fenced with Brass Nails, and made so
serviceable, that no ordinary Bullet, much less a Sword can
penetrate to injure them or their Masters, who have such
an artificial way of twisting themselves within the compass
of these shields that it is almost a vain attempt for their
enemy to annoy 'em." The targe is some 20 inches in
diameter, of two plys of oak, each ply made from three boards.
The cowhide covering was tooled and decorated with brass
studs. Fastened to the hide-covered back was a loop for
the arm and a hand grip. There may also be a holder for
the spike. The central brass boss sometimes has a hole
into which a ten-inch long spike was screwed, transforming
the targe into an actively defensive weapon. The seventeenth-
century targes have freer decoration, with the grotesque
animals seen on the brooches (p. 169) as well as interlacing,
while eighteenth-century targes are more stereotyped, often
with pierced brass plates as well as studs. It must be
admitted, however, that the Macdonald of Keppoch targe,

now in the Royal Scottish Museum, of eighteenth century date, is a masterpiece equal to those of the previous century.

To conclude, here is a short description of the Highland fighting man of 1715, from "The Loch Lomond Expedition": " James Grant, his son-in-law, Brother German to Brigadier Grant, followed by fourty or fifty stately Fellows in their short Hose and belted Plaids, and arm'd each of them with a well fix'd gun on his shoulder, a strong handsome Target, with a sharp pointed steel of above half an ell in length screw'd into the Navel of it, on his left arm, a sturdy Claymore by his side, and a Pistol or two with a Durk and Knife on his belt. . . ."

HIGHLAND DRESS

IN the space available this can hardly be more than an outline, with comments, on a subject which has occasioned more heat than light, and which still cries aloud for scholarly study, with very little response. The comments deliberately stress aspects which are considered to have been neglected elsewhere. The reader is recommended to turn to the chapter " The Highland Garb " in Sir Thomas Innes of Learney's edition of Johnston's " Clans, Septs and Regiments of the Scottish Highlands " (which quotes more of the relevant sources than any other work), McClintock and Dunbar's " Old Highland Dress and Tartans " (the only modern book on the subject with anything like an academic approach), D. W. Stewart's " The Setts of the Scottish Tartans " (the best work on tartans, with a valuable critical bibliography), and finally the articles on the subject by A. Haswell Miller. Much would be gained by an enquiry into the dress in its decline, or rather its resurrection, after the raising of the Proscription Act in 1782, along with the evidence of the papers and patterns of Messrs. Wilson of Bannockburn (the largest tartan manufacturers of that time) now practically all in public collections.

The few sixteenth-century references to the costume worn by those who inhabited the Highland area of Scotland are unanimous with regard to the striped or multi-coloured nature of their dress, the bare legs of the males and the wearing of a mantle and a saffron-coloured shirt, the mantle and the shirt said to be similar to those worn in Ireland. The saffron shirt, probably a straight-sided, linen garment, may not have survived long after the beginning of our period. An Irishman wrote in 1594 that the Highland auxiliaries in Ireland wore " a mottled garment with numerous colours hanging in folds to the calf of the leg, with a girdle round the loins over the garment." This appears to be a reference to what was later known as the belted plaid ; it must always be remembered, however, that the word " plaid " has had several meanings, from a horse-blanket to the shawl worn by a lady. It also referred to the cloth itself, sometimes known as " plaiding," a strong, woollen cloth, identified by one writer at the end of the eighteenth century as flannel. Tartan sometimes meant a self-coloured woollen cloth, and was so described by the Army as late as the eighteenth century. Thus two names for fabrics became a garment and a peculiar arrangement of coloured checks and stripes, as if the whole question of Highland dress was not complicated enough ! On the tartan question, let it suffice that there were no clan tartans in the modern sense until the second half of the eighteenth century, although certain colours and arrangements of colours may have been peculiar to certain districts, perhaps dependent on the availability of dyestuffs. Eighteenth-century portraits of Highland gentlemen wearing tartans of different designs at the same time prove conclusively that while a clan may have had certain colours which could be arranged at the discretion of the weaver, there was no such thing at that time as " one clan, one tartan."

There is not enough evidence to be dogmatic about how the plaid was worn before the end of the seventeenth century.

If one thinks in how many different ways a lady can wear a shawl, it will be appreciated what even a mere man could do with some ten yards of hard-wearing, woollen cloth which was part of his dress by day and his blanket at night.   To the end of the eighteenth century at least, a plaid of what has become known as " Shepherd's Tartan " (small checks of blue, black, green or brown on a light ground) was still worn by the older countrymen in the Lowlands, and worn very much as some earlier references to Highland dress describe it, as a wrap in bad weather, and in fine, either drawn round the waist or draped gracefully over the left shoulder.   When the plaid was cut in two, resulting in the waist-to-knee kilt as we have it today, is not known. J. Aston, valet to Charles I, wrote in 1639 of a Highland dress which was " like a pair of bases," i.e. like the pleated skirt often worn with sixteenth-century armour.   The portrait evidence (*see* Plate I and Fig. 22) is mainly of upper-class gentlemen, and it must be suspected that the artists could not resist adjusting the folds to suit either their sensibilities or their capabilities.   By the end of the seventeenth century the well-dressed Highlander was wearing his plaid in such a way that below his waistbelt it formed what we call a kilt, and above the waist it was worn either under or over his coat or jerkin.   This state of affairs continued to 1747, as is witnessed by Ramsay's portrait of the Earl of Loudon in the uniform of the Loudon Highlanders, and well beyond that date.   The story that the Englishman Rawlinson, manager of the Glengarry ironworks, was responsible (in the 1720s) for cutting the plaid and forming the " little kilt " is often repeated.   It is hard to believe, but it may be safely guessed that the belted plaid was abandoned because there was too much of it for comfort when worn under a

22. HIGHLAND
GENTLEMAN
c. 1700

coat. Man will endure much, but he will eventually put his comfort before tradition. The plaid was therefore either cut, or worn outside the coat. For comments on the fastening of the plaid, see page 170.

The modern kilt owes much to the Army. " If the wretched garment must have all those folds," one can imagine some Whitehall warrior saying, " for goodness' sake push them round the back and make them orderly and regular." It was probably a combination of military and Victorian modesty which gave birth to the ungainly long, mid-nineteenth-century civilian, and current Army, kilt. This is proved both by early references to the bare thighs of the Highlander and by the amusing French cartoons (*see* the Telfer Dunbar collection in Huntly House Museum, Edinburgh) of Scots soldiers in occupied Paris after the Napoleonic Wars, in which the Mademoiselles show their preference for the garb of old Gaul both as a model for their own fashions, and because of the exciting possibilities raised by a squad of kilties drilling in a high wind. Glasgow readers should consult the Wellington Monument, outside the Royal Exchange, to see how little the little kilt once was.

The Army is also responsible for perpetuating the monstrous horsehair sporrans, with shaving brush tassels, which appealed to early nineteenth-century Gothic taste. To be fair, the latest Army issues are, their blanco whiteness apart, much nearer the traditional sporran, which began as a leather purse with a thong as drawstring, and was looped over the belt (Fig. 23), and in the late seventeenth century followed the late medieval purse by becoming a leather or sealskin bag sewn to a brass top. The tops, often with cunning locks, were either rounded or angular ; one in the National Museum incorporates two small

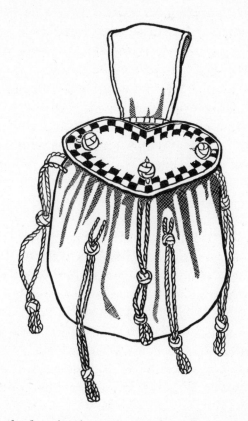

23. SPORRAN,
     SEVENTEENTH
     CENTURY

double-barrelled flintlock pistols to surprise the unwary
pick-purse.

Again, what the Army now calls trews, narrow tartan
trousers, are descended from the combined breeches and
stockings which were worn by Highlanders in the seventeenth
century, and in the eighteenth century appear to have
become an upper-class garment only, a somewhat rare
example (if indeed that was the case) of a fashion going up
in the social scale. The illustrations of eighteenth-century
trews show them to have been cut on the cross, as were

woven tartan stockings until recent times. Even the knitted stockings which succeeded them are diced in this manner. But we must not be too hard on the Army and its attitude to Highland dress. D. W. Stewart put forward a point of view with which many will agree when he wrote : "When the Highland regiments proved themselves among the finest fighting material in the British Army, so that the Scottish Nobility sought the honour of command in them, what might have come to be regarded as the barbarous if picturesque dress of a bygone age, remained to acquire an aura of military glory."

By the time the echoes of the '45 had died away and George III sat safely on his throne, the English observer, having overcome the feeling that " a hundred pipers an' a' an' a' " had once given him, was willing to accept the Highlander as a romantic figure. Even the Lowland Scot thought his dress well fitted to such a gallant fighting man now that the fighting was done away from the Lowlands. Boswell described a Skye gentleman in 1773 as " compleatly the figure of a gallant Highlander . . . he had his tartan plaid thrown about him, a large blue bonnet with a knot of black ribband like cockade, a brown short coat of a kind of duffil, a Tartan waistcoat with gold buttons and gold buttonholes, a bluish philibeg (kilt) and Tartan hose. He had jet black hair tied behind and was a large stately man." The Highlander of course had long known all this. Relating how he obtained his lieutenancy by persistent lobbying in Whitehall, Major John Macdonald gives the following picture of a Highland Ensign in 1762 : " I always appeared in my full Highland dress—that is a bonnet with a large bunch of feathers, great kilt, broadsword, pistol, dirk, large badger-skin purse and a pair of locks as big as besoms, with an amazing strut to set the whole off in the most marvellous manner. . . ."

But the great days of the dress, as of the weapons (*supra* p. 146) had gone. Raeburn's Highlanders, fine figures as they are, are fancy dress creatures. The Rev. I. Lettice, an English parson touring Scotland in 1792, put his finger on the problem and the answer when, after commenting that to see anyone dressed completely " in the old manner " was rare, since one wore " a hat instead of a Highland bonnet ; another puts on a Lowland coat upon his philabeg," he wrote : " When a Highlander begins to throw off any articles of his national dress, it is a pretty good pledge for his parting with the whole, as soon as he can with convenience equip himself in the English way ; for almost every mixture of the two dresses is so heterogeneous and has so much the appearance and effect of masquerade, that I am convinced, he feels something ridiculous in the air which it gives him, and no man loves to be long ridiculous."

The degeneracy of the dress was helped by the nineteenth-century practice of making the kilt from a much softer and thicker cloth than that previously used. The " hard " tartan, and the gentler, infinitely more pleasing natural dye colours of the eighteenth-century cloth made a much better kilt, as many modern manufacturers and wearers have discovered. It may have been that in earlier days the wool was combed, not carded, before spinning, giving a finer, stronger yarn. It was also the practice to use silk in weaving the finest eighteenth-century tartans. It may be added that the authors, after a study of photographs of Victorian gentlemen in kilts, have come to the conclusion that the sight of long, straggling whiskers over a hairy sporran—like a

goat above and a horse below—must have been too much
even for the Victorian onlooker, and it is little wonder that
the garb's next step was the music-hall stage, where it
almost perished altogether as a somewhat protracted joke.

Information about the dress of women in the Highlands
is almost non-existent. Lesley, in 1578, describes them as
wearing an embroidered gown to the ankles, under a mantle
of different colours, with bracelets and necklaces as their
chief ornaments. There is a gap of more than a hundred years,
with the exception of some scurrilous comments by English
writers, till Martin Martin, who is quoted in the section on
jewellery. Martin says the women wore a white plaid, with
" a few small stripes of black, blue and red." Several frag-
ments of cloth answering to this description exist in the various
collections. After discussing their brooches (the Highland
brooch described below, and another not identifiable), he goes
on : " The plad being pleated all round, was tied with a belt
below the breast. The belt was of leather and several
pieces of silver intermixed with the leather like a chain.
The lower end of the belt was a piece of plate, curiously
engraven, the end of which was adorned with fine stones or
pieces of coral. They wore sleeves of scarlet cloth, closed
at the end as men's vests, with gold lace round them, having
plate buttons set with fine stones. The headdress was a fine
kerchief of linen straight about the head, hanging down the
back taperwise. A large lock of their hair hangs down their
cheeks above the breast, the lower end tied with a knot
of ribbands." Later in the century dresses of woollen tartan
material were worn, made in the fashions of the Lowlands
(*see* Fig. 10).

JEWELLERY

THE connection between jewellery and costume is two-fold. In the first place the article of jewellery may be functional, for example a jewelled button or an enamelled brooch. The first brooches were dress fasteners, and they have retained that useful function, to a varying extent with changing fashions, as well as developing purely as ornaments. Secondly, the style of dress at a particular period determines what kind of jewellery may be worn. A diamond necklace loses much of its effect if worn on a high-necked gown, and an enamelled brooch would vanish against the background of a brightly embroidered fabric. Throughout the period and particularly towards its end, Scotland, as well as having a folk jewellery, participated in European fashions, the wealthy buying in France, Germany, Italy, Holland or England, while native goldsmiths also worked in European styles.

The materials used throughout did not vary to any great extent. Diamonds, sapphires, rubies and pearls were always popular, preferably in gold settings ; but whereas medieval stones were usually uncut and set en cabochon, square cutting was popular from the beginning of the period, and rose and other cutting in the seventeenth century. Brilliant cutting of diamonds was achieved about 1700. En cabochon stones are not found after the middle of the seventeenth century at latest.

Very few jewels made or worn in sixteenth-century Scotland still exist. There is evidence from inventories, however (notably that of Queen Mary, published by the Bannatyne Club), that the elaborate jewelled and enamelled bird- and beast-shaped brooches, the cameos, miniatures and the rest which Dr. Joan Evans has illustrated so well (*see* bibliography, p. 179) were worn in Scotland. The black silk doublets and gowns must have blazed with bright jewels, which were characterized by the magnificence of their intricate workmanship and the profusion in which they were worn. Most of the known jewels remain in private possession, but the enamelled gold locket containing her own and her son's pictures is one of the jewels of Mary, Queen of Scots, in the National Museum. The finest Scottish jewel of that time, the Lennox or Darnley jewel, made for Lady Margaret Douglas in memory of her husband the Earl of Lennox, who died in 1571, is now in the Royal collection. It is a heart-shaped gold pendant, richly enamelled on both sides with birds and flowers, and figures representing Faith, Hope, Victory and Truth, and set with a heart-shaped, cabochon sapphire and a jewelled crown. Heart and crown form the lids of compartments containing other emblems. In calling it a Scottish jewel it is not claimed that it was made in Scotland ; it is of importance, however, in that it was commissioned by a Scottish lady. Because of its symbolism and its enigmatic emblems, Dr. Evans has said that it is " unique in its abstruseness and complexity." It is however, typical of its period in the way in which, despite the elegance of its workmanship, the forceful design and colour, helped by the crudity to our eyes of its stone settings, give it a life and vigour which is absent in the jewels of later years.

The heart symbolism is repeated in another jewel of the period, an enamelled gold locket set with rubies and emeralds and bearing a portrait cameo of Queen Mary. Dr. Evans has suggested that this may be of Scottish workmanship ; she also illustrates two other portrait cameos of the Queen. This love of the heart shape found expression again and again in the succeeding centuries.

Portraits of before *circa* 1650 show that costume, including hats, was decorated with smaller jewels in a way which has not been repeated since, although the semi-functional jewels which adorned late seventeenth-century gowns (*see* p. 59) might also be put in that class. In general, seventeenth century interest lay in precious stones for themselves, in their size and in their cutting. Men became less interested in jewellery, apart from rings. Sir John Foulis, himself the grandson of a goldsmith, does not mention one item of jewellery in his voluminous accounts for the period between 1671 and 1707. No doubt the religious temper of the time had much to do with this. The plain silks of ladies' gowns towards the end of the century meant that jewellery could be quieter than before and still attract attention. The mid-century garnet-set silver jewel shown in Fig. 24B illustrates the emphasis on abstract design which was characteristic. The original on which the drawing is based is on loan in the National Museum.

The goldsmiths soon found other ways of expressing themselves. Watch cases had been their province since their introduction in the sixteenth century ; the earliest watches were, in fact, treated as pieces of jewellery and shared the naturalistic forms of their time. Later watches, notably those of David Ramsay, a Scot who went south with James VI and became Keeper of his clocks and watches, were more like the ones we know today, although the decoration of their elaborate cases proclaims them also to be personal ornaments as much as timepieces. Engraved silver and gold watch covers were popular early in the seventeenth century, followed by pierced gold and silver covers, and about mid-century by delicate gold filigree work. Enamelling was also popular for watch cases. The seventeenth century saw the rise to popularity of the medal in Britain, and many examples of the medallist's art, particularly the medallions and lockets made as memorials for Charles I and as propaganda pieces, rank as jewellery, or at least as costume accessories.

Another form of jewellery closely connected with the Stewart cause was the neck or wrist slide, the earliest of which date from Charles II's reign, but which, judging by dated examples, seem to have been popular in Scotland as jewellery between 1690 and 1710. Almost oval in shape and about an inch, or less, in length, their flat-topped rose-cut crystals are set in gold or silver, with either plain gold or enamelled backs. The settings usually have a toothed edge, which is characteristic of the period. Under the crystal, on plaited hair or coloured silk, are elaborate monograms in fine gold wire or tiny, painted china figures and emblems. As well as commemorating the deaths of members of the Royal family (Orange as well as Stewart) and of private persons, they also celebrated marriages with appropriate symbols—cupids, hearts with arrows through them and the like. They occur in pairs, suggesting that they were exchanged on marriage. Sometimes they have pearl or precious stone borders. How they were worn is a mystery which portraits do not elucidate. The two loops at the back suggest that they were worn on ribbons at neck or wrist.

There are also pendants similar to the slides in style and sometimes heart-shaped.

Silver chains, presumably of the type on Midside Maggie's Girdle in the National Museum, are often mentioned in late sixteenth- and seventeenth-century inventories and served a variety of purposes. They are prominent in portraits of the period. The Girdle mentioned dates to 1608–9, but it acquired its romantic story when it was given to Margaret Hardie of Midside Farm by Lord Lauderdale as a reward for her loyalty in continuing payment of the rent of her farm when he was in prison after the battle of Worcester.

Scottish jewellery in the eighteenth and nineteenth centuries was either the same as that of England and France or, rarely, it influenced the fashions of these countries. The use of polished pebbles in the jewellery of this period may have a Scottish origin. Sleeve-links and rings set with pebbles are known to have had Scottish owners, and as early as the 1750s the loss of " Scotch pebble buttons " was advertised in the Norwich Mercury newspaper. Sliced, polished pebbles and agates were also used as·decoration on eighteenth-century French (or English) chatelaines. The revival of interest in seals and cameos in the later eighteenth-century also meant the use of semi-precious stones. Brooches set with Scottish amethysts and cairngorms, often with a thistle as witness to their Scottish origin, were popular in the 1820s. They are definitely lighter in conception, and more attractive in design, than their Victorian successors, although not all of these are heavy and lifeless. Sometimes their use of contrasting colours and the fine markings of the stones is excellent. There was a great vogue for " Scotch pebbles " in the middle of the nineteenth century, especially when Queen Victoria showed interest in them, but not all pebble

brooches are Scottish in origin or in manufacture.   Some
of the finest brooches, in characteristic " Celtic " designs
were made in Devon, for Scotland has no monopoly of
attractive stones.   Unfortunately it is the exception to find
a nineteenth-century brooch which has been marked either
with the maker's name or the date letter.   Again it is difficult
to say whether the eighteenth-century brooches and pendants
set with garnets are Scottish or French.   Certainly there has
long been a liking here for these attractive stones, sometimes
known as " Scotch rubies."

The use of cairngorms (" the Scotch topaz ") coincided
with the interest in things Highland which began after the
echoes of the '45 had died away and was fostered by Sir
Walter Scott's novels and poems and by George IV's visit
to Scotland in 1822.   Not only did this result in the dress
weapons of the time acquiring stone settings (the tops of
dirks and skean dhus), but the traditional round brooch
of the Highlands was given a cairngorm centre.   The history
of this brooch goes back well before our period, and it
illustrates probably better than most things the Highlander's
amazing conservatism, his ability to go on using the same
article and to give it a twist which made it all his own.

In twelfth-century Europe tunics were fastened at the
neck by round brooches, having simple pins without catches.
The two corners of the tunic neck were pulled through the
ring of the brooch and the pin skewered through prepared
holes in the tunic.   Thus a fastening akin to that of the peg
of a modern duffle coat was achieved, with the peg taking
the place of the pin and the buttonhole that of the brooch,
the only difference being that the pin was hinged to the
brooch at one end.   Later, changing fashions and materials
called for a brooch fastening that was safer and less harsh on

fine fabrics. On Highland materials, however, it remained suitable and the Gael saw no reason to change. The silver brooches found in Scotland with hoards of coins which date them to the thirteenth and fourteenth centuries gave place to bronze or brass as they moved down the social scale, but there is a recognizable chain of development in the ornamentation of the flat surface of these brooches, from the earliest down to the eighteenth century. The chain is weak in the sixteenth century and it is difficult to date accurately certain brooches which must come from that time, but when the Highland brass brooch has fully developed in the seventeenth century the sequence becomes clear.

Martin Martin, in his description of the Western Isles about 1700, describes how the arisaid, the white plaid of the women, was " tied before on the breast with a buckle of silver or brass, according to the quality of the wearer." Some were " as broad as any ordinary pewter plate," he added ; brass brooches of eight inches in diameter are known, their faces engraved in panels and roundels with grotesque animals and leaves and basketwork designs as Martin described them. Note that he calls them buckles, a very accurate description when you think of the way in which the tongue of a buckle fastens a leather strap through a prepared hole, and remember that Martin was not accustomed to seeing brooches with that type of fastening. A few silver brooches with grotesque animals included in their decoration have survived, seventeenth century in date if not earlier, but early in the eighteenth century the designs of both silver and brass brooches degenerated, as did those of other Highland things. The engraving became lighter, the animals gave way entirely to crude foliage decoration, hatching and scrolls. Thistles appear on later eighteenth-

C—12

century examples and the series ended with crude, undecorated circles of bronze or copper, often with iron pins,
mere fasteners, and in no way ornamental. The pin of
circa 1700 has a barrel-shaped end, split longitudinally and
forced over a narrowed portion where the ends of the ring
join. In the early 1700s there appeared for a short time a
silver version of the round brooch, engraved and decorated
with the black sulphur compound, niello. These appear to
have been made by town jewellers and not by individual
Highlanders or by tinker craftsmen, " wandering jewellers "
they should perhaps be called. The decoration of these
silver brooches is heavy, many having a curious anchor-like
device without ancestry in the earlier brooches.

It was this round brooch which, with the addition of a
central cairngorm, became, during the Highland dress
revival of the nineteenth century, the shoulder fastening for
the plaid. There is a precedent for the addition of the
centrepiece, for it was a recognized medieval variation of
the round brooch—the great reliquary brooches, such as the
Brooch of Lorne, are essentially of this type—but there is no
pictorial or written evidence, so far as is known, for fastening
the man's plaid on the shoulder. Martin expressly says that
the women fastened their plaids on the breast with round
brooches, while the men used a toggle or pin. Perhaps the
reader would care to experiment in fastening two thicknesses
(at least) of tartan cloth, one on top of the other, not edge to
edge and without prepared holes, on the left shoulder, with
a circular brooch which has a fairly blunt-ended pin and no
safety-catch.

This pin is also found on the eighteenth-century heart
brooch, the brooch which is often called a " Luckenbooth,"
because it was sold in the Luckenbooths (locked booths)

24. JEWELLERY

A. SILVER HEART BROOCH, MID EIGHTEENTH CENTURY

B. JEWEL, SILVER AND GARNETS, SEVENTEENTH CENTURY

C. HEART BROOCH, GARNET MOUNTED, *c.* 1820

D. ENGRAVED HEART BROOCH OF SILVER, *c.* 1850

E and F. SILVER HEART BROOCHES, LATE EIGHTEENTH CENTURY

which formed the jewellers' quarter around St. Giles Kirk in Edinburgh. Another name (for there are many) is " Queen Mary Brooch," but there is no connection between the plain silver heart of the eighteenth century and the heart-shaped jewels of the Queen's time already described. Sometimes the heart is crowned, and sometimes two hearts are entwined under a crown, giving a form not unlike a crowned M, and it may be this which has caused the identification with Queen Mary. They appear to have been popular in both Highlands and Lowlands, although they are con- spicuously absent in the pictorial and written sources of the period. Inscriptions (on the backs) prove that they were often love tokens—" My heart is thine and thine I crave," " Wrong not the heart whose joy thou art " and " Ruth 1 and 16." The Bible-reading Scots girl of the eighteenth century would not need to be told that the verse includes the words : " Whither thou goest, I will go; and where thou lodgest, I will lodge." Probably the lack of evidence of their being worn (for they have survived in fair quantity) is explained by the fact that they have a connection with the protection of a newborn child—the custom is recorded of pinning a heart brooch on a baby's shawl. They are essentially female possessions, handed down in families in the female line. Copper and bronze brooches have survived, and a few of gold, but most are of silver, the late eighteenth- century examples often bearing the marks of those travelling silversmiths about whom too little in known. Such men as Charles Jamieson and the Alexander Stewarts seem to have used the marks of the town where they were staying at the time. Many of the best brooches have been collected in Aberdeenshire, an area which has been rich and self- contained for a long time, which took the middle line at the

Reformation, and which has preserved examples of many of the old arts and crafts and traditions, from fine woodwork to old ballads. One has the impression that, from the seventeenth century, Aberdeenshire folk have spent the long winter evenings making brooches and powder horns and songs, and not in arguing religion and politics as in districts to the south.

Late in the century the heart brooch took on an eighteenth-century classical look ; it became larger, with stylized ornament on its shoulders and at its point. In some ways these are the finest of the type, even when they lack the individuality of the earlier ones. Early in the nineteenth century the surface was engraved, and before mid-century set with coloured paste. These are jeweller-made brooches, not folk jewellery. In a sense they are degenerate specimens, but there are very attractive examples in which the whole outline is formed by garnets. About this time also the old fastening gave place to the modern safety-catch, and many older brooches have had their pins removed and new ones substituted.

Information about what rings were worn is not easy to find. In portraits of the sixteenth century both men and women wear rings, on all fingers and on the thumbs, but the number of Scottish portraits is too small to learn much from the few rings that are painted in sufficient detail to be examined. Elaborate gem cutting did not become a possibility until this time, and many of the rings of the period had " en cabochon " settings, the stones being rounded and without facets, their bezels consequently being irregularly shaped. The few rings which survive have a charming simplicity coming from a flowing or plastic use of the gold setting unlike later work. Portraits also show

square, oblong and lozenge-shaped bezels, set with simply
cut stones. Inventories of the seventeenth century rarely
give sufficiently detailed information to allow us to picture
the rings, and it became conventional for artists from the
mid-seventeenth to the end of the eighteenth century not to
include rings in portraits. Nor have rings a high survival
value. If they contained valuable stones it is quite possible
that successive generations have thought them worthy of new
settings more in keeping with the fashion of the time. And if
they were not valuable enough to be worth changing, they
were not worth keeping. Happily there are a number of
dated rings to guide us. Much information must come from
rings with historic associations or from chance finds which
correspond in style to these. Generally speaking, changes
in rings have lain in the cutting of the stones, the seventeenth-
century innovation of having several stones in separate
settings (small diamonds round a larger one, for instance)
and in the increasing decoration of the shoulders of the hoop.

A number of rings are associated with Mary, Queen of
Scots, of which two, both in national museums, are of
importance. The signet ring in the British Museum had her
arms engraved on a crystal, the heraldic metals and tinctures
being applied on the inside of the oval bezel, on a blue
ground, and appearing through the crystal. The shoulders
are ornamented with flowers and leaves, once enamelled.
The gold pendant in the National Museum of Antiquities,
probably made for the Queen, bears arms similar to those
on the ring. The pendant has an outer enamelled border
set with four diamonds ; an enamelled gold drop hangs
from a loop below the border. Both ring and pendant are
almost certainly French, the ring dating to before 1558.
What appears to be a betrothal ring, bearing the initials of

Mary and Darnley (M and H joined over a true lover's knot), and " Henri L. Darnley " and the 1565 date, with a crown and a lion rampant shield, engraved behind the circular bezel, is in the Victoria and Albert Museum. Copies of this ring, which is said to have been found near Fotheringhay Castle, have been made for many years, and regularly appear at Museums as exciting finds ! Signet rings with crystal settings may not have been common in Scotland (they appear on English portraits), but in the second half of the eighteenth century the native semi-precious stones and polished pebbles were very popular for signets, usually heraldic, and also for the classical cameos which were fashionable at that time. Signet rings were certainly popular in late medieval times, bearing both coats of arms and merchants' marks. These were usually plain gold or silver rings with flat bezels, heavier and cruder editions of the Mary and Darnley ring.

One result of the Scottish preoccupation with memorials to the dead has already been mentioned, the slides of *circa* 1700 ; another was the mourning ring, given by the deceased's family to his (or her) friends, often according to instructions in the will, in order to keep his memory alive. This custom has its roots far back in European tradition. Again we know the seventeenth- and eighteenth-century types best from royal commemorative rings. Those of the mid-seventeenth century had narrow hoops and often relatively large bezels, containing, say, a miniature of the deceased under glass, or more rarely under a table-cut diamond. Hoops continued narrow until the end of the century. The workmanship (often French in surviving examples) improved and the shoulders (on either side of the bezel) were decorated, either bifurcating (as sometimes

they had done before), with curling arms which held the
bezels, or widening to carry enamelled designs. Smaller
stones were often set between the forks. The style of some of
these rings is very like that of the slides—the same rounded
bezels with toothed edges, containing under crystals the same
skulls and crossed bones on plaited hair. The hair of the
deceased remained a prominent feature of all *memento mori*
jewellery throughout the nineteenth century, in rings, lockets
and brooches. By the 1820s the somewhat gruesome
bracelets and rings of plaited hair had appeared. There
was a fashion after the middle of the eighteenth century,
and into the nineteenth, for broad-hooped rings without
bezels, usually with the dead man's name and dates reserved
in gold on black enamel. Sometimes the inside was inscribed (engraved on the gold), and the outside of the heavy
ring had cut decoration between black borders. About
1770 memorial rings with large, pointed oval bezels (over
an inch long in cases) were popular. They contained, under
glass, hair and certain emblems. These were eighteenth-
century classical in origin—urns, with or without weeping
women drooping over them, broken columns, and the like,
either painted or in the round, in the shape of gold or
porcelain figures. A distinction must be made between the
rings issued to a large number of mourners, a seventeenth-
century and earlier custom which survived in the
eighteenth century, and personal memorials, such as we have
been describing, made for, and worn by, close relatives and
friends. Presumably the former were much simpler and
cheaper.

Inscriptions reserved in gold on enamel have been
mentioned. This technique, both for inscriptions and other
decoration, was popular in French jewellery early in the

eighteenth century, and a number of the memorial rings
associated with the Jacobite Rising of 1745–6 are decorated
and inscribed in this manner. These may have been made
in France, but there is a tradition that at least one of them
was made by a Scottish goldsmith. They include the
mourning ring for Lord Lovat, another which commemorates
Lovat and other Jacobites (including Kilmarnock and
Balmerino) executed in the Tower of London, and a Jacobite
propaganda ring having in its bezel a small gold medallion
bearing the head of Prince Charles Edward. The hoops of
these rings are carved and decorated all round, with
inscriptions reserved in gold on enamel, and two have a
thistle between the forks of one shoulder and a rose in the
other. All three, along with a similar ring commemorating
a private individual and dated a few years later, are at
present in the National Museum.

A plain gold, eighteenth-century wedding or betrothal
ring in the National Museum is inscribed, " Quhair this I
give, I wiss to live," an inscription reminiscent of those on
heart brooches, and of the late medieval European posy
rings. The makers of the heart brooches also made engage-
ment rings, of silver, bearing a plain, flat, heart-shaped
bezel, inscribed with the girl's initials. The nineteenth-
century fashion for polished stone jewellery does not seem
to have affected rings, and the period closes without there
being distinctively Scottish examples.

SOURCES

THIS is not a comprehensive bibliography, but rather a guide to the chief sources from which the book has been written.

The main source of illustrative material has been the files of the Scottish National Portrait Gallery, which include photographs of pictures not in the collection as well as many engravings. Published illustrative sources are few and in no way comprehensive, consisting as they do of catalogues and books on individual artists. Kay's *Portraits* (the edition of 1877) is an outstanding exception readily available to anyone interested. Sculpture, including seventeenth- and eighteenth-century churchyard monuments and sundials, has proved valuable. Actual costume has been studied in the National Museum of Antiquities of Scotland, in local museums and in private houses.

We have had access to unpublished written sources in the course of our work, and we should like to stress how much there is worthy of publication, particularly as the trend is for societies publishing historical material not to be interested in such things.

The principal printed sources are contained in the publications of the various societies—the Scottish Text Society, the Scottish History Society, the Spalding Club, the Society of Antiquaries of Scotland and the Burgh Records Society; in the Reports of the Historical Manuscripts

Commission and in official publications by the Scottish Record Office, a particularly valuable one being the Lord High Treasurer's Accounts. For the early years there are P. Hume Brown's *Early Travellers in Scotland* and R. Chambers' *Domestic Annals* (to 1745). John Ramsay of Ochtertyre's *Scotland and Scotsmen in the Eighteenth Century*, E. D. Dunbar's *Social Life in Former Days* and the Rev. John Mitchell's *Memoirs of Ayrshire about 1780* (Scottish History Society, Miscellany vol. vi) are particularly valuable for the eighteenth century. The best guide to other sources for that period is the bibliography of the relevant chapter in Marjorie Plant's *Domestic Life in Eighteenth Century Scotland*. For the early years of the nineteenth century, when the real flood of sources is beginning, the *Memoirs of Susan Sibbald* (edited by F. P. Hett) is valuable. For military dress, the recent publication of *The Uniforms and History of the Scottish Regiments* by R. M. Barnes and C. K. Allen, fills a gap. Joan Evans's *A History of Jewellery*, 1100–1870, is an excellent survey of European jewellery; there is a valuable section on Scottish hand firearms in H. J. Jackson and C. E. White-law's *European Hand Firearms of the 16th, 17th and 18th Centuries*.

INDEX